Planning Your Financial Future
Study Guide

Steven L. Christian
Barbara H. Luck
Jackson Community College

LOUIS E. BOONE
University of South Alabama

DAVID L. KURTZ
University of Arkansas

DOUGLAS HEARTH
University of Arkansas

THE DRYDEN PRESS

HARCOURT BRACE COLLEGE PUBLISHERS

FORT WORTH PHILADELPHIA SAN DIEGO NEW YORK ORLANDO AUSTIN SAN ANTONIO
TORONTO MONTREAL LONDON SYDNEY TOKYO

Address for Editorial Correspondence
Harcourt Brace College Publishers, 301 Commerce Street, Suite 3700, Fort Worth, TX 76102

Address for Orders
Harcourt Brace & Company, 6277 Sea Harbor Drive, Orlando, FL 32887
1-800-782-4479

ISBN: 0-03-018422-3

Printed in the United States of America

6 7 8 9 0 1 2 3 4 5   095   9 8 7 6 5 4 3 2 1

The Dryden Press
Harcourt Brace College Publishers

Preface

How To Use Your Study Guide

The intent of the student study guide is to support your learning. No new content is meant to be added but you may discover a different process to learn or apply the material from the textbook.

We suggest that the study guide be used in an interactive fashion with the text and classroom activities, instead of waiting until completion of the chapter to utilize the study guide.

Each chapter of the study guide contains six activities:

Activity 1:   What Do You Know?

Activity 2:   Chapter Overview

Activity 3:   Chapter Outline

Activity 4:   Key Terminology Exercise

Activity 5:   Multiple Choice Questions

Activity 6:   Experiential Problems

Activity 1:   What Do You Know?

Before you read each chapter or listen to a lecture, answer the questions in this section. This will help you develop an "anticipatory mind-set" or simply help you begin to focus on the new material. Some of the questions are objective and a single correct answer exists. Other questions are subjective which will require a personal opinion or value judgment, and will differ from person to person. Identifying your feelings, thoughts, and habits is a good place to start your study in each of the areas of personal finance. Relax and enjoy this section.

Activity 2:   Chapter Overview

The chapter overview provides a simple one paragraph preview of the chapter. By combining with the "What Do You Know?" activity you have taken the most important step to prepare yourself to digest large amounts of detailed information. Don't skip these steps!

Activity 3:   Chapter Outline

The chapter outline may be used either as a note-taking guide during classroom activities or as a means of organizing questions that arise during the reading of the text.

Harcourt Brace & Company

Activity 4: Key Terminology

Using the fill-in-the-blank, matching, crossword puzzles, or word searches will develop your ability to recognize these words outside of the classroom setting. In addition, you will develop your skill in actually using the terminology as you conduct your personal financial business. The benefits of the key terminology exercises can be realized at any time throughout your study of the chapter.

Activity 5: Multiple Choice Questions

Use the multiple choice questions to measure your mastery of the concepts in each chapter. This activity is beneficial if used near the completion of the material studied. Try this activity with the textbook closed, then refer to the answer key upon completion of all questions. Discovering incorrect answers should prompt you to refer to the text.

Activity 6: Experiential Problems

These experiential problems will bridge the gap between classroom theory and real world application. All are elements of a person's financial plan and implementation for success. Some may be more applicable depending upon your age, family situation, or career stage. These problems vary in length and complexity. Many require that you venture off campus. The problems are specifically designed to create interaction with the people, places, and events encountered in a lifelong personal financial plan and its implementation.

Harcourt Brace & Company

Contents

Harcourt Brace & Company

Part 1

Personal Financial Planning

Chapter 1   **An Overview of Personal Finance**

Chapter 2   **Career Aspects of Personal Finance**

Chapter 3   **Developing Financial Statements, Plans, and Budgets**

Chapter 1

An Overview of Personal Finance

What Do You Know?

Before you begin reading Chapter 1: Overview of Personal Financial Planning, answer the following questions to assess your knowledge, skills, and abilities of personal finance as of today. Relax and enjoy. This is just to see where you are starting.

  T   F   1.   Young people do not need to budget or save money.

  T   F   2.   The stock market scares me.

  T   F   3.   I am not completely satisfied with my standard of living.

  T   F   4.   I don't pay off my credit card balances each month.

  T   F   5.   Life insurance is the most important savings/investment I can do for my family/children/spouse.

  T   F   6.   Money left over after the bills are paid is the only money available for savings/investment.

  T   F   7.   I need to do a financial plan.

  T   F   8.   I worry about getting/keeping a good paying job.

  T   F   9.   The best place to save money is in a savings account at the bank.

  T   F   10.   When I retire my company pension and Social Security will take care of my needs.

Chapter 1

An Overview of Personal Finance

Chapter Overview

Personal finance is the study of the economic factors and personal decisions that affect a person's financial well-being. Personal finance involves learning about money as well as examining the way we live our daily lives. Critical changes in our world have dramatically increased the importance of understanding personal finance today. Financial goals evolve and change as your age and lifestyle change which makes personal finance a subject you will study all through your life. Part 1 will assist you with goal-setting which is the beginning of any sound financial plan.

Chapter Outline

I.   The Meaning and Importance of Personal Finance

    A. Improvement in one's standard of living

    B. Personal finance determines our lifestyle OR our lifestyle determines our personal finance

    C. Sluggish growth in personal income increase

    D. Expect to change jobs several times

    E. Overwhelming number of choices in all aspects of personal finance from banking to car loans to retirement planning

    F. Making financial goals and decisions occurs throughout your life

II. A Personal Financial Management Model

    A. Begins with knowing:

        1. values - what is important to you
        2. goals - what you hope to save
        3. priorities - ranking the values and goals in importance and urgency

    B. Separate personal goals

        1. short term
        2. long term
        3. non-monetary

    C. Each goal must be specific, contain a deadline, and be defined as a result.

D. Financial planning includes:

1. career choice

2. cash and credit management

   a. prepare a budget
   b. select the right bank
   c. establish a regular savings plan
   d. obtain credit
   e. compute finance charges
   f. repair a poor credit history

3. tax planning

   a. federal income tax
   b. state income tax
   c. sales tax
   d. property tax

4. buying

5. insurance

6. investing

7. retirement

E. Personal financial plans will be affected by:

1. government policy (taxes and regulations), examples may be:

   a. changes to Social Security
   b. mandatory auto insurance coverage
   c. changes to Federally Insured Student Loan Program

2. economic conditions

   a. business cycle stages
      1) prosperity
      2) decline
      3) recession
      4) recovery

   b. stage of business cycle determined by
      1) unemployment
      2) inflation
      3) interest rates

III. Developing A Financial Plan

A. Make decisions that contribute to your making more money

1. on the job

2. through investments

B. Make decisions to save more and spend less

C. Know where you spend money

IV. The Time Value of Money

A. Means that $1 today is not equal in value to $1 one year from today

B. $1 loan to a friend would be influenced by:

1. inflation - the value of $1 one year from now may be $.97
2. opportunity costs - the $1 loaned to a friend would not be earning interest in your savings account
3. risk - you must be compensated for taking the chance that your $1 may not be returned to you

C. There are two ways to apply the time value theory of money:

1. future value - you have an amount of money today and you want to know its worth in the future
2. present value - you know how much you'll have in the future, and you want to know its worth today

Name _____   Instructor _____

Date _____   Section _____

Key Terminology Exercise - Fill In

Using the terms from the Running Glossary in your text complete the following statements.

1. If you divide the number of people looking for a job by the total number of people in the work force you have the_____.

2. _____ is the most widely accepted measure of a country's economic performance.

3. The income that you have left after paying your taxes is your _____.

4. The process of _____ is used to find what an amount of money in the future is worth today.

5. If you invest a sum of money today, its value in 10 years is call its

    _____.

6. The kind of car you drive, the neighborhood you reside in and the kind of vacation you take are all expressions of your _____.

7. When businesses are hiring and everybody is working is the opposite phase of the _____ to when businesses are laying off and people are out of work.

8. When the price of gas goes up it may be caused by _____ which is usually measured by the _____.

9. The income that you have left after paying you taxes and for food, clothing and shelter is

    _____.

10. _____ will make your invested money grow faster than _____ because you are earning interest on your interest.

11. Driving a newer car, living in a bigger house and eating more expensive food would indicate that your _____ has increased.

12. Your _____ is the total money that you get in salary, interest, dividends and from all other sources.

13. If you are offered $100 in five years and you wish to know what it is worth today you are attempting to find the _____.

14. The rent that you pay to use someone's money is called _____.

15. The interest that you would lose if you withdrew your money from your savings account and invested it in a mutual fund is a(n) _____.

Name _____   Instructor _____

Date _____   Section _____

Multiple Choice Questions

1. Economists predict that over the next 10 or 20 years personal income will
    a. increase greatly.
    b. decrease greatly.
    c. increase slightly.
    d. decrease slightly.

2. The decline in job security make sound personal financial management
    a. more important than ever before.
    b. less important than it used to be.
    c. too difficult to even attempt.
    d. no more important than before.

3. Personal financial management is an important activity
    a. for people under 20 years old.
    b. for people 20 - 40 years old.
    c. for people over 40 years old.
    d. for people of any age.

4. To develop a good financial plan, one must first have a good understanding of one's
    a. values.
    b. goals.
    c. priorities.
    d. a, b and c

5. Which of the following was/were mentioned as step(s) in developing a financial plan?
    a. maximizing income and wealth
    b. using money more effectively
    c. monitoring expenditures
    d. all of the above

6. Financial goals should be reviewed periodically and reflect changes in
    a. education.
    b. family situations.
    c. emotional well-being.
    d. all of the above

7. Over the next 20 to 30 years people should plan to depend
    a. more on savings and less on Social Security.
    b. less on savings and more on Social Security.
    c. about the same on each.
    d. on neither one.

8. During a recession consumers are more likely to be
   a. optimistic.
   b. pessimistic.
   c. ambivalent.
   d. unaffected.

9. Disposable personal income is the amount left after
   a. all necessary living expenses have been paid.
   b. taxes are paid.
   c. taxes and all necessary living expenses have been paid.
   d. nothing has been paid.

10. The index most widely used as a measure of inflation is
    a. Gross Domestic Product.
    b. personal income.
    c. Consumer Price Index.
    d. National Monetary Index.

11. In the United States the supply of money and credit is controlled by
    a. Congress.
    b. the banking systems.
    c. the President.
    d. the Federal Reserve Board.

12. Which of the following is **not** a consequence of poor financial planning?
    a. hard to improve ones standard of living
    b. mounting debts
    c. general inability to make ends meet
    d. all of the above

13. All of the following are basic reasons for the time value of money **except**
    a. risk of not getting your money back.
    b. opportunity cost.
    c. sunk cost.
    d. risk of inflation.

14. If you invested $500 for 10 years at 9%, how much would you have?
    a. $950.00   c. $1,183.70
    b. $5,451.48   d. $450.00

15. If you invested $200 at 5% simple interest for two years, how much would you have?
    a. $220.25   c. $205.00
    b. $220.00   d. $210.00

16. If you invested $200 at 5% compound interest for two years, how much would you have?
    a. $220.25   c. $205.00
    b. $220.00   d. $210.00

17. If a person wished to have $1,000 in five years and could invest money at 6%, how much would he or she have to invest now?
    a. $700
    b. $940
    c. $747.30
    d. $850.90

18. Using the "Rule of 72", how many years will it take to double your money at 9%?
    a. 8
    b. 9
    c. 18
    d. 5.78

19. You would earn more interest if the compounding were done
    a. yearly
    b. quarterly.
    c. monthly.
    d. it would not make any difference, they are the same.

20. You are given the following three options
    1) $95.33 today
    2) $50 in six months and another $50 in one year.
    3) $102.95 in one year.

    If you can invest your money at 8%, which is the best option?
    a. option 1
    b. option 2
    c. option 3
    d. it would not make any difference, they are the same

Name _____   Instructor _____

Date _____   Section _____

Experiential Problems

1. Read the local newspaper for five days (they do not need to be consecutive). As you read the paper look for articles that answer the following questions:

   a. What stage of the business cycle is your local community currently experiencing?

   b. List three indicators mentioned in the articles that led you to your conclusion.

   c. Explain how each indicator mentioned in part b impacts you personally.

2. Think of someone you know who is 40 years or older and has set financial goals. Ask that person if he/she will spend 15-20 minutes with you sharing and discussing his/her financial goals. During your interview ask the following questions:

    a. What are your financial goals?

    b. Talk me through the process or thoughts you had in developing these goals.

c. How have your goals changed over the years and why?

d. Who, personally or professionally, assisted you in developing or revising your goals?

e. What resources (books, newspaper, continuing education courses) did you find most helpful in developing or revising your financial goals?

f.   What parting words of wisdom can you give me?

3.   One of the most important steps in any good financial plan is the goal-setting process. In order for you to be successful, these goals must be based upon your values.

This exercise is designed to take you through the process of creating personal financial goals.

A.   Identify personal values.

B.   Brainstorm financial goals.

C.   Reconcile values to goals.

D.   Write goal statements.

A. Identify personal values

    1. Read ''values'' sheet on page 1-14.

    2. Check those values which apply to you.

    3. Select the three most important to you.

    4. Rank those three in order of importance.

    most important _____

    second most important _____

    third most important _____

B. Brainstorm financial goals

List 10 things you dream about having or doing.

    1. _____

    2. _____

    3. _____

    4. _____

    5. _____

    6. _____

    7. _____

    8. _____

    9. _____

    10. _____

Harcourt Brace & Company

Value Sheet

Here is a list of values that you might identify for yourself. It is not an all-inclusive list so if you identify any other personal values, feel free to add them.

accomplishment - being results-oriented

aesthetics - an appreciation of beautiful things

altruism - helping others with the anticipation of no reward

ambition - desire to get ahead (however you desire to "get ahead")

creativity - ability to develop new, innovate things or ideas

environment - concern for the health of the planet

freedom - lack of restraints

friends and associates - enjoy being surrounded by

health and physical fitness - taking care of your mind and body

intellectual stimulation - excited by knowledge and learning

inner peace - acceptance of what is

marriage and family - primary focus of your life

monetary reward - put a dollar value on your decisions

recognition - people notice what you've done

responsibility - willingness to accept consequences of actions

risk - do you enjoy uncertainty?

self-respect - caring what you think of yourself

security - lack of uncertainty; predictability

social justice - everybody gets treated fairly

social respect - caring what others think of you

status - the right car, the right job, the right neighborhood

stuff - prizing of gadgets, toys, material possessions

C. Look at the "dream sheet" you created in step B. Eliminate those dreams that are inconsistent with the values that you identified in step A. For example, if one of your values is prestige, and one of your dreams is to drive a new BMW, this is consistent. However, if prestige was not one of your values driving a BMW may be an inconsistent goal.

List the remaining dreams that are consistent with your values in the space provided. (You may not use all the spaces provided.)

1. _____
2. _____
3. _____
4. _____
5. _____
6. _____
7. _____
8. _____
9. _____
10. _____

D. Write goal statements

Now you are ready to turn your dreams into reality by writing goals. Goals must be:

1. results-oriented
2. action words
3. time-specific
4. measurable
5. realistic yet challenging

Refer to p.1-18 of the study guide. Fill in the goal worksheet columns as you read through steps 1-5 below.

1 and 2.   Results-oriented and action words. Results are the outcomes; what you will have when you have achieved your goal. Examples are a college degree, a house, a car, a computer, a savings account, a trip around the world, spring break in (wherever).

Action words are used to ensure that you do something. Here are some examples:

establish	create	initiate
buy	consult	investigate
contribute	analyze	organize
evaluate	estimate	participate

Fill in the first column of the worksheet labeled "brief description". Combine an action word with a result. For example:

Brief Description
(action word)   (result)
Buy a computer

Fill in the second column of the worksheet labeled "Actions to be Taken". Again combine an action word with a result. These are intermediate goals used to achieve the primary goal.

Actions to be Taken
(action word)   (result)
Open a savings account
Contribute $10 a week to it

3.   Time-specific. Establish a date by which you wish to have the goal achieved.

Target Date for Completion
2 years

4.   Measurable. This can be difficult to calculate for some goals but without it, it will be impossible to know when the goal has been met.

Estimated Cost
$1,250

5.   Realistic. Do not set yourself up for failure. Goals need to be challenging but realistic. While it may seem attractive to earn a four year degree in two years, do you have the time, money and energy to take 35 credit hours per term?

The final column on your work sheet is labeled "Priority." Rank each goal as high, medium or low. Now refer back to part a of this exercise and compare the values you identified to the identification and ranking of your goals. Answer the following questions:

1. Are there any values for which you have established no goals?

2. Are the priorities of the values consistent with the priorities of the goals?

Worksheet
Your Personal Financial Goals

Name(s)_____   Date Prepared _____

Short-Term Monetary Goals (One Year or Less)

Brief Description	Actions to Be Taken	Target Date for Completion	Estimated Cost	Priority

Long-Term Monetary Goals (Five Years or Less)

Brief Description	Actions to Be Taken	Target Date for Completion	Estimated Cost	Priority

Nonmonetary Goals

Brief Description	Actions to Be Taken	Target Date for Completion

Chapter 1 Solutions

What Do You Know?

The more "trues" you circle, the wiser was your choice in signing up for this class.

Key Terminology Exercise - Fill In

1. unemployment rate
2. gross domestic product (GDP)
3. disposable personal income
4. discounting
5. future value
6. lifestyle
7. business cycle
8. inflation, consumer price index (CPI)
9. discretionary personal income
10. compound interest, simple interest
11. standard of living
12. personal income
13. present value
14. interest
15. opportunity cost

Multiple Choice Questions

1. c		11. d
2. a		12. d
3. d		13. c
4. d		14. c*
5. d		15. b*
6. d		16. a*
7. a		17. c*
8. b		18. a*
9. b		19. c
10. c		20. d*

*Calculations for Multiple Choice Questions:

14. ($500 x 2.5937) - Future Value of $1
15. ($200 + [$200 x .05 x 2])
16. ($200 x 1.1025) - Future Value of $1
17. ($1000 x .7473) - Present Value of $1
18. (72÷9)

20. Option 1 $95.33

    Option 2   ($50 x .9806) + ($50 x .9259) - Present Value of $1

    Option 3   ($102.95 x .9259) - Present Value of $1

Chapter 2

Career Aspects of Personal Finance

What Do You Know?

T F 1. During a job interview, men and women tend to react in a similar fashion.

T F 2. Help wanted ads are one of the best places to find a job.

T F 3. Millions of employed people work at home on a full- or part-time basis.

T F 4. Half of all businesses fail within two years of opening.

T F 5. After being established in a career, your need for education is pretty much over.

T F 6. Many experts predict that job growth will come from large corporations, rather than small companies.

T F 7. Employment in the manufacturing sector is expected to decline over the next 10 years.

T F 8. Twenty years ago, college students listed ''develop a meaningful philosophy of life'' as the most important reason for going to college.

T F 9. When discussing salary in a job interview, try to indicate what you'll need before the company makes the offer.

T F 10. Computerized scholarship services are usually a good source of assistance when you need a list of financial aid sources.

Chapter 2

Career Aspects of Personal Finance

Chapter Overview

Your personal financial situation is largely determined by the career you choose. Your career and income are largely determined by the amount of education you have. Financing that education is the second most expensive purchase for most people, particularly since education is now considered to be a life-long activity. Choosing a career requires not only taking a personal inventory, but also doing a considerable amount of research on industrial, occupational, and geographic growth and trends. Finally, the job search needs to be managed as thoroughly and seriously as you have managed your college career.

Chapter Outline

I. Career Choice and Personal Goals

    A. Money and financial security more important now than 20 years ago

    B. Job satisfaction includes intellectual challenge, pleasant work environment, and friendly co-workers

    C. Social contribution is defined as making a difference to our planet and its people

II. Variables that Affect Your Income Potential

    A. Education - the more you get, the higher your earnings and the lower your unemployment

    B. Financing your education - second most expensive life purchase

        1. federal government
            a. loans
            b. grants
            c. work-study
        2. private loans
        3. scholarships
            a. federal
            b. state
            c. corporate
            d. non-profit
        4. cooperative education programs

C. Continuing education

D. Occupational earning patterns

III. How To Choose A Career

A. Take a personal inventory

1. define your career goals
2. explore your career interests
3. identify your skills, abilities, and specialized knowledge
4. apply your educational background to the job market
5. analyze each job you have ever had
6. explore your hobbies and personal interests

B. Consult a vocational counselor

C. Research job growth in major occupational areas

D. How to measure career potential

1. industry's growth prospects
2. occupation's growth prospects
3. job location
4. employer's growth prospects

E. Consider other roads

1. prepare for an occupational cluster
2. think about working for yourself
3. look at telecommuting

F. Sources of career information

IV. The Job Search

A. Where to look

1. friends, acquaintances, relatives
2. campus career office
3. public and private employment offices
4. professional associations
5. newspapers
6. trade publications
7. electronic bulletin boards
8. direct contact with employers

B. How to write an effective resume

1. need a job objective or career goal
2. state past experience as skills
3. look beyond structured job experiences to identify your skills
4. one page limit
5. choose a specific format
    a. chronological
    b. functional
    c. targeted

C. Cover letters

1. <u>always</u> include with a resume
2. write from employer perspective
3. don't use form letter
4. limit to 4-5 paragraphs and one page

D. Handling the interview

1. first impressions are critical
2. preparation is the key
3. demonstrate strength and self-confidence
4. remember to ask, not just answer, key questions

E. Deciding on a job

1. may be called back for a hiring interview
2. must consciously decide if:
    a. the job meets your career goals
    b. the financial package is acceptable
    c. the work environment and you are compatable

F. Reentering the workforce

Name _____   Instructor _____

Date _____   Section _____

Key Terminology Exercise - Crossword Puzzle

Using the words found in the Running Glossary, complete the crossword puzzle. An X indicates a space between words in a multi-word answer.

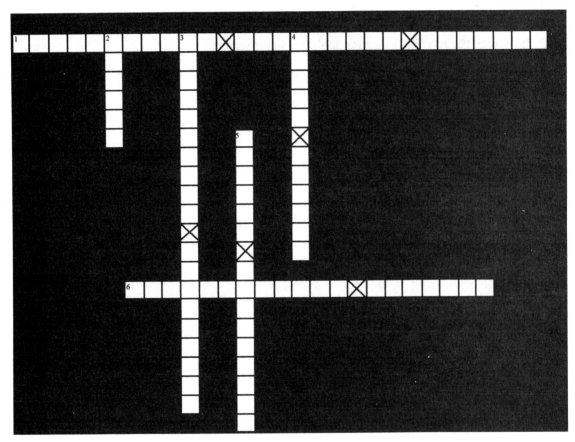

Across

1. This offers a student a chance to go to school one term and work the next in a job related to the student's major.
6. A group of related jobs.

Down

2. When applying for a job you would send out this document which details your education and work experience.
3. If you wish to know what careers and occupations your skills and background make you best suited for, seek the advice of this person.
4. This document attempts to sell your skills and abilities and accompanies the document in 2 down.
5. When a company wishes to downsize without laying workers off but by not replacing people who die, retire or leave for other reasons, they are relying on this.

Name _____   Instructor _____

Date _____   Section _____

Multiple Choice Questions

1. In choosing a career the most important consideration should be
    a. the amount of money you can earn.
    b. how much you love the work.
    c. how prestigious the job.
    d. how well the job fits your personal goals and values.

2. The earnings gap between a college graduate with a bachelor's degree and a high school graduate
    a. has widened.
    b. has narrowed.
    c. has remained the same.
    d. no longer exists.

3. The cost of a college education in relation to inflation is
    a. not rising as fast.
    b. rising at the same rate.
    c. rising faster.
    d. no longer not rising at all.

4. Which of the following is a way to finance you education?
    a. Pell Grants.
    b. Federal Work Study.
    c. PLUS Loans.
    d. all of the above

5. The U.S. Department of Labor projects that the biggest growth in employment to the year 2005 will be in the
    a. services area.
    b. government.
    c. manufacturing.
    d. mining.

6. The worst area(s) for job growth today is
    a. California.
    b. Northeastern states.
    c. both a and b
    d. neither a nor b

7. To become more marketable and less susceptible to economic downturns you should
    a. specialize in one career.
    b. prepare for a group of related jobs.
    c. prepared for jobs in several unrelated areas.
    d. none of the above

8. One of the factors to be considered in being self-employed is that your earnings can be
    a. very high.
    b. very low.
    c. both a and b
    d. stable.

9. In your job search you should
    a. tell relatives, friends and acquaintances you are looking for a job.
    b. visit the campus career planning and placement office.
    c. read local newspapers and trade publications.
    d. all of the above

10. Which of the following should **not** be included on your resume?
    a. your name, address, and phone number
    b. your family history
    c. your job objective
    d. your educational and work background

11. Resumes should be
    a. limited to one page.
    b. 1 to 3 pages.
    c. 3 to 5 pages.
    d. no less than 5 pages.

12. Which of the following is **not** a resume format?
    a. chronological
    b. step-by-step
    c. functional
    d. targeted

13. A cover letter should be written to
    a. convince the employer to grant you an interview.
    b. provide additional information not found in the resume.
    c. tell the employer what you can do for their company.
    d. a and c

14. A cover letter should
    a. grab the attention of the reader.
    b. sell yourself.
    c. invite a call to action.
    d. all of the above

15. To prepare for an interview you should
    a. study the firm's annual report.
    b. prepare questions to ask the interviewer.
    c. have the proper clothes for the interview.
    d. all of the above

16. You should take the job that
    a. offers the best salary.
    b. offers the best fringe benefits.
    c. offers the best fit to the factors in your decision framework.
    d. offers the best job location.

Name _____ Instructor _____

Date _____ Section _____

Experiential Problems

1. Listed below are 15 personal values which may be taken into consideration when choosing a career. Rank these values as they relate to you. Use 1 for the most important and 15 for the least important.

☐ **Achievement**
Accomplishment: a result brought about by resolve, persistence, endeavor.

☐ **Altruism**
The regard for or devotion to the interests of others.

☐ **Associates**
Working with people you find congenial and enjoyable.

☐ **Creativity**
The creation of new and innovative ideas and designs.

☐ **Economic Return**
Salary, wages, and benefits obtained from a job.

☐ **Independence**
To work alone; to make one's own decisions; to have little or no supervision.

☐ **Intellectual Stimulation**
Learning for the sake of knowledge; seeking information or principles to satisfy one's curiosity or for the power of knowing.

☐ **Management**
Organizing people or tasks; having control of an organization or unit.

☐ **Physical Abilities**
To be able to use one's body and its strength to accomplish one's job; to use one's hands to manipulate or to create; technical expertise.

☐ **Prestige**
To feel significant and important; to have recognition; to believe that people have high regard for this type of job.

☐ **Risk**
What one does is more important than the security of the job.

☐ **Security**
To want security from the job regardless of the type of work or work setting.

☐ **Surroundings**
Working environment is very important; could include outdoors, pollution, carpeted offices, and facilities.

☐ **Variety**
To have non-routine tasks and assignments; to have each day vary.

☐ **Way of Life**
To work as one chooses without a need to conform in dress, personal philosophy, hobbies and other activities.

2. The two best ways to find jobs are through personal referrals and direct contacts with employers. (See Exhibit 2.7 textbook page 47) Employment agencies and want ads are the least successful methods.

Networking is the way to make referrals and direct contacts occur. One way to network is through conducting informational interviews.

An informational interview is a face-to-face meeting with someone who has knowledge, insights, and experiences that may be of value to you. It is not a job interview. Informational interviews are not typically done with people you know. Those people are already in your network and presumably the benefits from a relationship with them have already been realized. You are looking for ways to increase the quantity and quality of the contacts and referrals within your existing network.

Before the information interview:

A. Determine the Topic

   -accounting field

   -owning a business

   -management jobs

   -company XYZ

   -service industries

B. Determine the objectives

   -By the end of the interview, I will have an awareness of what it takes to work for Company XYZ, a major employer in town, as well as be able to describe the company culture.

   -By the end of the interview, I will be able to describe a typical day for a manager of a bank.

   -By the end of the interview, I will know the basic steps to follow to open a business.

C. Outline the interview format. Draft a list of possible questions according to your stated objectives. Examples include:

What is the best way to get started in this occupation?

What sorts of changes are occurring in your field?

What do you like best about your job? least?

Describe a typical day.

What college courses helped you the most?

List the five critical skills necessary for success.

Would you please estimate the salary ranges for your occupation? job title?

What professional organizations, affiliations, or social responsibilities are beneficial to support this type of career?

Describe the kinds of decisions as well as problems you encounter.

What advice would you have for someone in my position or situation?

Which personality traits and characteristics best describe someone in this field? company? job?

Describe the work environment for this occupation or company.

Who is your hero? mentor?

How did you come to work here? in this field? geographic location?

Where will you be in 5 years? 10 years?

Which company is your major competitor? In what do they excel?

What are some time management techniques that are helpful?

Describe a stressful situation relative to your work.

How do you react to these types of situations?

How do you balance work, home, spirituality, mental and physical well-being? Prioritize these if you would.

D. Select the company and/or the person for the interview. If you are particularly fond of a certain company, start with that company. If you favor a particular occupation, start there.

Use your current network of family, friend, fellow students, families and friends of fellow students, neighbors, professors, places with whom you do business, church, local news stories from radio and newspapers to find local successes, etc.

When you request an interview, explain that you are a student at _____, and why you would like an appointment with them. Specify the amount of time needed (be brief) and give an example of the kind of question you will ask.

E. Research the person, occupation, industry, and company. You want to impress this person with your preparedness for the interview.

During the interview:

A. Have a "dry run" if possible so you know time and distance to the company, parking arrangements, entrance locations.

B. Dress appropriately.

C. Arrive a few minutes early.

D. Arrive with your notes and questions prepared in a folder or notebook.

E. Be gracious to others, e.g. secretary, technicians, security, cafeteria employees.

F. Be prepared to answer questions about your professional goals and experience.

G. Don't go beyond the agreed time; however, be prepared to have the interview extended by the interviewee.

H. Thank everyone connected with this interview.

After the interview:

A. Write up your thoughts and interviewee's responses immediately.

B. Send a thank you letter/note the same day.

3. Refer back to the ranking of your personal values in experiential problem #1 and answer the following questions:

   a. Does the career that I am considering coincide or conflict with my personal values?

   b. Are the conflicts (if they exist) significant?

   c. What should I do to eliminate these conflicts, e.g. rethink the ranking of my personal values, rethink my career choice?

Chapter 2 Solutions

What Do You Know?

1.	F	6.	F
2.	F	7.	T
3.	T	8.	T
4.	T	9.	F
5.	F	10.	F

Key Terminology Exercise - Crossword Puzzle

Across

1. cooperative education program
6. occupational cluster

Down

2. resume
3. vocational counselor
4. cover letter
5. worker attrition

Multiple Choice Questions

1.	d	9.	d
2.	a	10.	b
3.	c	11.	a
4.	d	12.	b
5.	a	13.	d
6.	c	14.	d
7.	b	15.	d
8.	c	16.	c

Chapter 3

Developing Financial Statements, Plans, and Budgets

What Do You Know?

T F   1. People with low incomes have more difficulty managing money than people with high incomes.

T F   2. Personal financial statements, such as the income statement and balance sheet, are just a lot of busywork and have more value for the person with a lot of money.

T F   3. I usually see a doctor to diagnose my physical health but I have never seen a financial planner to diagnose my financial health.

T F   4. I balance my checkbook when I feel like it and that is usually less than 4-6 times per year.

T F   5. The best investments are a house and a savings account, and are all that you really need.

T F   6. A good financial plan will prevent me from enjoying life.

T F   7. Budgeting has been a nightmare for me.

T F   8. If I ever complete a financial plan, I'll be relieved that I'll never have to do that again.

T F   9. I think I overspend.

T F   10. If I encountered an unexpected emergency that cost me $400, I know how I would pay it.

Chapter 3

Developing Financial Statements, Plans, and Budgets

Chapter Overview

Financial planning begins with an understanding of your values or what is important to you and good records which provide up-to-date accurate information. With this foundation you can begin the financial planning process which will lead to the development of a financial plan. Two fairly immediate goals will then be to establish an emergency fund and acquire adequate insurance. A budget will be developed to monitor and control expenses.

Chapter Outline

I. Personal Financial Statements

    A. The income statement - flow of income and expenses

        1. salary and wages

        2. taxes

        3. housing expenses

        4. food and clothing

        5. transportation

        6. medical expenses and child care

        7. savings

    B. Balance sheet - what you owe and own

        1. current assets - cash, checking and savings accounts

        2. long-term financial assets - retirement, 401(k) accounts

        3. fixed assets - house, cars, personal property

        4. current liabilities - utility and credit card bills

        5. long-term liabilities - mortgage, care and student loans

        6. net worth - equals assets minus liabilities

    C. Monitoring Your Financial Position

        1. financial ratios - benchmarks

        2. liquidity ratio - how much cash could you put in your pocket today in case of an emergency

        3. debt-to-total asset ratio - your ability to pay your debts

4. debt service ratio - percent income for debt repayment

5. financial assets to net worth - percent of net worth made up of stocks, bonds, mutual funds, cash, savings accounts, retirements accounts

II. Financial Planning

    A. Step 1: Values are the foundation

        1. What is important to you?

        2. What would you like to accomplish in your life?

    B. Step 2: Establish goals consistent with your values

        1. Where do you want to be in 5-10 years?

           a. monetary goals

           b. non-monetary goals

        2. Where do you want to be in 6-12 months?

           a. monetary goals

           b. non-monetary goals

    C. Step 3: Develop strategies to achieve your goals

        1. Strategies need to be consistent

        2. Strategies need to be logical

        3. Strategies need to be realistic

    D. Financial planning is done with estimates and assumptions you must make based on information you have as a result of life-long learning.

    E. Goals and strategies will change as you go through various life stages, however your values will remain fairly constant.

III. Preliminary Budget Concerns

    A. Set up an emergency fund

        1. size depends on fringe benefits

        2. typically 3-6 months income

        3. may require self-discipline and self-denial to meet this goal

    B. Purchase adequate insurance

        1. life

        2. health and disability

        3. property and liability

IV. Budgeting

   A. Budget

      1. short-term financial plan
      2. prepared on a monthly basis
      3. tracks expenses in order to meet short and long term goals
      4. helps reduce impulse buying
      5. all household members should participate
      6. should not deprive you of what you need

   B. Budget components

      1. cash flow - equals income minus expenses
      2. fixed expenses stay the same, e.g. rent
      3. variable expenses fluctuate, e.g. food

   C. Budget format

      1. estimated income
      2. actual income
      3. estimated expenses
      4. actual expenses
      5. variances - differences between estimated and actual
      6. monthly totals
      7. lack of planning and impulse buying will destroy a budget
      8. keep it simple

   D. Completing the budget form

   E. Consumer spending patterns

      1. average U.S. household spends $30,000 per year
      2. housing   = 32%
      3. taxes   = 18%
      4. transportation = 18%
      5. food   = 14%
      6. varies with age of household

V. Record Keeping

    A. Where should records be kept?

        1. file card system for names, addresses, phone of key people such as attorney, accountant, etc.
        2. home filing cabinet for less important records
        3. safe-deposit box for stock certificates, real estate deeds, birth certificates, passports
        4. personal computer for financial records

    B. How long should records be kept?

Name _____   Instructor _____

Date _____   Section _____

Key Terminology Exercise - Fill In

Using the terms from the Running Glossary in your text, complete the following statements.

1. Automobiles, houses, savings accounts, mutual funds and 401(k) plans are examples of your _____ while the unpaid balances on student loans, home mortgages, VISA cards and car loans are examples of your _____ and both are shown on your _____.

2. The salary, interest, dividends and other money you receive is your _____ or sometimes referred to as _____ while your house and care payment, food and other money you pay out is your _____ or sometimes referred to as _____ and are both shown on your _____.

3. If you want to know where you stand financially at any given point in time, the best thing to do is to prepare _____.

4. _____ is the amount that the current value of what you own exceeds the current amount that you owe.

5. You wish to own your own home at 30, send your children to Podunk U., and retire at 50 so you develop a _____ to help reach these goals.

6. The process of deciding what actions you must take to reach your goals is called _____.

7. When you keep track of what you earn and spend you are _____ so that you can compare this information to your financial plan.

8. The relationship of your assets and liabilities is a measure of your ability to pay your debts called _____.

9. A savings account that is equal to three to six months living expenses and will be used if you have a loss of income is a(n) _____.

10. Last month you budgeted $150 for entertainment but actually spent $250 for a _____ of $100.

11. If your paycheck plus other sources of money exceed your spending, you have positive _____.

12. Should your TV blow up, the price of the new TV is the _____.

Name _____   Instructor _____

Date _____   Section _____

Multiple Choice Questions

1. Financial statements will do all of the following **except**
   a. provide up-to-date evaluation of your financial well-being.
   b. guarantee that you will get loans.
   c. provide a starting point for estate planning.
   d. detect potential financial problems.

2. The percentage of Americans who regularly balance their checkbooks is
   a. almost 100%.
   b. more than 75%.
   c. less than 50%.
   d. almost nobody balances their checkbook regularly.

3. In determining your total income for budgeting purposes which of the following should you include
   a. wages and salary.
   b. interest and dividends.
   c. bonus and profit sharing.
   d. all of the above

4. The budget category where most people have the most difficulty accounting for how/where they spent the money is
   a. housing.
   b. vacation and entertainment.
   c. cash allowances.
   d. miscellaneous.

5. The statement where a person's assets and liabilities are shown is called the
   a. balance sheet.
   b. income statement.
   c. cash flow statement.
   d. retained earnings statement.

6. Items which can quickly be converted into cash are called
   a. long-term financial assets.
   b. fixed assets.
   c. net worth.
   d. current financial assets.

7. Almost half of all households ratio of net worth to annual income is
    a. about 1 to 1.
    b. about 2 to 1.
    c. about 1 to 2.
    d. less than 1 to 2.

8. Numerical benchmarks that give you an indication of your current financial position are
    a. financial statements
    b. financial ratios
    c. financial plans
    d. financial goals

9. Most experts suggest that you should have enough liquid assets to provide living expenses for
    a. 1 to 3 months.
    b. 3 to 6 months.
    c. 6 to 9 months.
    d. 9 to 12 months.

10. Lenders may not extend additional credit if the percentage of loan payments to take home pay exceeds
    a. 40%.
    b. 30%.
    c. 20%.
    d. 10%.

11. All of the following are financial strategies **except**
    a. increasing the amount you are putting into your 401(k).
    b. shifting your portfolio to higher yielding mutual funds.
    c. planning to retire at 50.
    d. buying vacant land and selling it later to a developer for a profit.

12. In order to make your financial goals more attainable you should
    a. put a time frame on each.
    b. estimate the cost of achieving the goal.
    c. develop a strategy to reach the goal.
    d. all of the above

13. Which of the following would typically not be a financial goal of a younger person?
    a. buying a house
    b. paying off educational loans
    c. estate planning
    d. saving for child's education

14. A budget should do all of the following **except**
    a. permit you to track expenditures.
    b. avoid impulse purchases.
    c. stop you from buying something you need.
    d. help you reach longer-term obligations.

15. All of the following are examples of variable expenses **except**
    a. food.
    b. gas and electric bill.
    c. entertainment and vacation.
    d. car payments.

16. Budgets should be formatted to show
    a. budgeted and actual income.
    b. budgeted and actual expenses.
    c. variance.
    d. all of the above

17. The largest single expenditure category for U.S. households is
    a. personal and Social Security taxes.
    b. housing.
    c. transportation.
    d. food.

18. People tend to overspend because
    a. they carry too much cash.
    b. they want to ''keep up with the Joneses.''
    c. they use credit cards.
    d. all of the above

19. Old tax returns should be kept
    a. forever.
    b. three years.
    c. seven years.
    d. one year.

Name _____   Instructor _____

Date _____   Section _____

Experiential Problems

1. Complete the worksheet on pg 3-12. Compare the goals you identified to the goals and values you identified in experiential problem #3 in chapter 1. Based on your comparison answer the following questions:

    a. Are the goals on the chapter 3 worksheet different from the goals on the chapter 1 worksheet? List the differences.

    b. Do any of the goals on the chapter 3 worksheet not coincide with the values you identified in chapter 1? List those goals that do not coincide.

    c. Are there similarities between your list in part a and b?

d. Review the goals that do not coincide and briefly discuss how they do not coincide with your top three values.

e. Based on what you determined by your analysis in part d, revise your values or goals worksheet.

WORKSHEET
Your Financial Plan

Goal	Time Frame	Estimated Cost of Dollar Goal	Strategy
A. Spending			
1.			
2.			
3.			
B. Debt			
1.			
2.			
3.			
C. Investments			
1.			
2.			
3.			
D. Insurance			
1.			
2.			
3.			
E. Other Personal Goals			
1.			
2.			
3.			

Harcourt Brace & Company

2. Identify where you are on the life cycle of financial planning (Exhibit 3.7 in the text).

   Develop at least three financial goals that you feel will be important to you for each of the next three steps in the life cycle. Be sure to keep your values (refer back to chapter 1) in mind as you develop your goals.

3. Prepare a budget for your cash expenditures for a two-week period. Without referring to your budget keep a log of every cash expenditure that you make during the two-week period. Use a notebook or note pad small enough to carry with you at all times. Do not attempt to record all expenditures at the end of the day; you will forget some. Record the date, nature of expenditure (pizza, beer, video rental) and amount.

At the end of the two weeks summarize the expenditures in your log into the categories you used in your cash budget for the period. Now compare your actual and budgeted expenditures. Answer the following questions:

a. Did you overspend in any category? List those in which you did. (If you did not overspend in any category - CONGRATULATIONS - take the rest of the night off.)

b. Referring to the "Advice of the Experts" box in your text, identify a reason you overspent. (Your reason may not be on the list.)

c. Based on the reasons you identified in part b develop a strategy for each that will help you reduce or eliminate the overspending in the future.

Chapter 3 Solutions

What Do You Know?

1. F
2. F
3. F
4. F
5. F
6. F
7. F
8. F
9. F (most people do not think they do)
10. T

Key Terminology Exercise - Fill In

1. assets, liabilities, balance sheet
2. income, cash inflows
   expenses, cash outflows
   income statement
3. financial statements
4. net worth
5. financial plan
6. financial planning
7. budgeting
8. solvency
9. emergency fund
10. variance
11. cash flow
12. replacement cost

Multiple Choice Questions

1. b
2. c
3. d
4. c
5. a
6. d
7. d
8. b
9. b
10. a
11. c
12. d
13. c
14. c
15. d
16. d
17. b
18. d
19. a

Part 2

Managing Your Money

Chapter 4

Money Management

What Do You Know?

T F 1. I chose the particular bank for my checking and/or savings account simply because my parents have accounts there.

T F 2. I don't have enough money for a savings account therefore I don't have one.

T F 3. I earn interest on my checking account.

T F 4. My bank does not charge to use an ATM owned by my bank and only up to $1.00 if the ATM is owned by another bank. (If you don't know, answer false.)

T F 5. I shopped around for the bank with the lowest fees for the services I use.

T F 6. I can name and explain 4 services my bank offers.

T F 7. A bank savings account is the only real option for a savings plan.

T F 8. All financial institutions offer the same services.

T F 9. Stopping payment on a check is easy to do and inexpensive.

T F 10. I do not write many checks so there is no need to reconcile my account each month.

Chapter 4

Money Management

Chapter Overview

''Keep it under the mattress'' or ''bury it in the backyard'' are no longer common options to money management. Most of us have a checking and/or savings account. It is the safest way we can get to our money easily and quickly. However, choosing the best option is an individual decision that requires a bit of time and effort. Understanding how money grows as well as the fees charged to handle your money are two concepts of critical importance.

Chapter Outline

I. The Roles of Money Management and Savings

    A. Why maintain cash balances - convenience

    B. Why is savings so important

        1. emergencies

        2. specific goals - home, college, vacation, retirement

    C. Setting savings goals

        1. emergencies - 3-6 months of after tax income

        2. short-term goals - divide $ amount needed by time available

        3. long-term goals - divide $ amount needed by time available

        4. determine regular amount to save and treat as a required expense

        5. set up automatic transfer from checking to savings each month

    D. What determines how fast your savings will grow

        1. frequency of compounding

        2. treatment of deposits and withdrawals

II. Choosing The Right Place For Your Money

    A. How important is convenience

    B. What services do you expect

    C. How much does it cost - banks now charge high fees for services

    D. What insurance safeguards are present

III. The Services Offered by Financial Institutions

    A. What are the major financial institutions

        1. commercial banks - full service bank

        2. savings banks or savings and loan associations - resemble commercial banks

        3. credit unions - cooperatively owned by borrowers and depositors

        4. brokerage firm - central asset management accounts

    B. Checking accounts

        1. regular - maintain a specified minimum balance or pay a monthly service charge

        2. special - monthly fee and per-check fee

        3. overdraft protection

    C. NOW accounts or Share-draft accounts

    D. Consumer loans

    E. Bank credit cards

    F. Other banking services

        1. retirement plans

        2. trustee services

        3. safe-deposit boxes

        4. bank wire transfers

        5. debt management and counseling

    G. Electronic banking

        1. automated teller machines (ATMs)

        2. debit cards and point-of-sale transfers

        3. preauthorized payments and transfers

        4. home banking

        5. safety of electronic funds transfer systems

IV. Using A Checking Account

    A. How to open and maintain an account

        1. signature cards

        2. account number

        3. record keeping

    B. Making deposits

   C. When and how to stop payment on a check

   D. How to write and endorse a check

   E. Balancing your checkbook

   F. Certified checks and chashier's checks

   G. Traveler's checks

IV. Savings Options

   A. Savings accounts

      1. non-fixed time deposits
      2. fixed-time deposits

   B. Money market mutual funds

      1. not federally insured
      2. very safe
      3. interest varies with market interest rates
      4. minimum initial deposit
      5. checks limited to $250 or more

   C. U.S. Treasury bills and notes

      1. securities backed by U.S. Treasury
      2. safe
      3. can be sold prior to maturity
      4. market interest rates
      5. exempt from state and local taxes
      6. purchase directly or from brokerage firm

   D. U.S. savings bonds

      1. purchase prive ifs half of bond value
      2. exempt from state and local taxes
      3. federal tax deferred

   E. Choosing the best savings option

Name _____   Instructor _____

Date _____   Section _____

Key Terminology Exercise - Matching

Match the words in column A to the statements in column B. Not all of the words in column A will be used.

Column A

A. Nominal rate of interest
B. Effective rate of interest
C. Continuous compounding
D. Day of deposit to day of withdrawal
E. NOW account
F. Bouncing a check
G. Blank endorsement
H. Restrictive endorsement
I. Special endorsement
J. Third party check
K. Certified check
L. Cashier's check
M. Passbook (statement) savings account
N. Money market deposit account
O. Certificate of deposit
P. Money market mutual fund
Q. Treasury bill
R. Treasury note
S. Savings bond
T. Electronic funds transfer (EFT) system

Column B

___ 1. Similiar to a money order except you purchase this from a bank and it is drawn on the bank's general funds.

___ 2. A debt of the government sold through the U.S. Treasury with an intermediate maturity (2 to 10 years).

___ 3. The bank advertises this as the interest rate paid on savings accounts.

___ 4. This method for computing interest will produce the highest effective rate.

___ 5. To prevent further endorsing or negatiation of a check use this.

___ 6. A place to put your savings that will give you higher interest than a passbook account but ties your money up for a set period of time to get the higher interest.

___ 7. The method used for computing (annually, quarterly, etc) will determine this rate.

___ 8. Considered to be the safest investment in the world and owned by millions of Americans.

___ 9. The most common way to endorse a check.

___ 10. A way to earn interest on your money that has the fewest restrictions; is easy to understand but does not pay much interest.

___ 11. When you endorse a check from your dad to your roommate to reimburse him for the rent he paid, the check becomes this.

___ 12. If you forget to deposit your paycheck before writing checks this will happen.

___ 13. A quick way to get your money from point A to point B using modern technology.

___ 14. You are concerned whether the check given to you has money in the account to cover it, so you ask the individual to have the bank guarantee payment.

___ 15. Short term (less than 1 year) U.S. Treasury security.

Name _____   Instructor _____

Date _____   Section _____

Multiple Choice Questions

1. If you bounce a check the average fee you can expect is
    a. $5
    b. $15
    c. $25
    d. $50

2. Opening a checking account for today's consumer is
    a. complicated.
    b. expensive.
    c. both a and b
    d. neither a nor b if you make the right choice.

3. The most common reason why people keep cash is
    a. they do not trust banks.
    b. it is convenient.
    c. they like to run their fingers through it.
    d. so that their significant other cannot check the bank statement and track their expenditures.

4. Which of the following is not a reason why people save money?
    a. ensure that you have funds that are quickly convertible to cash
    b. to provide an emergency fund
    c. for a vacation
    d. all of the above

5. A persons need for savings is determined by his/her
    a. short term financial goals
    b. long term financial goals
    c. both a and b
    d. neither a nor b

6. Which of the following is the actual interest that you will earn?
    a. effective rate of interest
    b. legal rate of interest
    c. stated rate of interest
    d. nominal rate of interest

7. The difference in the effective rate of interest resulting from continuous compounding as opposed to daily is
   a. significant.
   b. slight.
   c. no effect.
   d. depends on the rate.

8. The fairest way financial institutions can employ to compute interest is based on
   a. average daily balance.
   b. exact number of days the money is in the account.
   c. high balance during the month.
   d. low balance during the month.

9. Since deregulation, financial institutions have
   a. eliminated many free services.
   b. offer more free services.
   c. raised fees on other services.
   d. a and c, only

10. Which of the following will not lower your banking costs?
    a. shopping around
    b. not begging
    c. reading the fine print on your monthly statement
    d. asking your bank if they have a better deal

11. Putting your money in a financial institution that is not federally insured is
    a. never a good idea.
    b. O.K. if the institution has a long, safe history.
    c. O.K. for some but not all of your money.
    d. a matter of personal choice.

12. Which of the following does **not** offer banking services?
    a. credit unions
    b. some large retail stores (e.g. Sears)
    c. brokerage firms
    d. savings and loan associations

13. Which of the following **cannot** be used like a checking account?
    a. central asset account
    b. NOW account
    c. share-draft account
    d. they can all be

14. Debit cards
    a. can be used in ATM machines.
    b. deduct a purchase from your bank account.
    c. give you the option to finance a purchase.
    d. a and b, only

15. One of the problems with electronic banking is
    a. it is much harder to make deposits.
    b. it is much harder to make withdrawals.
    c. it is impossible to stop payment on a check.
    d. all of the above

16. You should balance your checkbook monthly because
    a. you may have made an error in writing or recording a check.
    b. the bank may have made an error.
    c. someone may have altered a check you wrote to raise the amount.
    d. all of the above

17. Which of the following will guarantee that a check will be good?
    a. having the person giving you the check write ''payment guaranteed'' in the memo part of the check
    b. having the person giving you the check show you their most recent bank statement
    c. getting a check that is stamped ''certified by the bank''
    d. checking the person's Dun and Bradstreet rating

18. A savings account where the interest rate varies with the market interest rate is a
    a. statement savings account.
    b. NOW account.
    c. money market deposit account.
    d. certificate of deposit.

Name _____   Instructor _____

Date _____   Section _____

Experiential Problems

1. Exhibit 4.6 from page 129 in your text is reproduced below. The information for each criteria/instrument has been omitted.

Exhibit 4.6
Comparing the Major Savings Options

Instrument / Criteria	Statement Savings and NOW Accounts	Bank CDs	U.S. Treasury Issues	Money Market Mutual Funds	Bank Money Market Accounts
Minimum Investment					
Liquidity					
Yield					
Safety					
Taxation					
Summary					

Write these phrases in their proper place(s) in the grid. A choice may be used more than once.

1. Federally insured up to $100,000
2. Specified maturities
3. Interest taxable at federal, state and local levels
4. Vary
5. Can withdraw money without penalty
6. Varies from bank to bank
7. Rates set at banks discretion
8. Safe or generally safe
9. Convenient to get at or Easy access to funds
10. Flexible in choice of maturities

2. The four people listed here have come to you seeking advice on where to put their savings. Each has given you certain facts about their particular situation. Using this information and that provided in Exhibit 4.6 in your text advise them as to the most appropriate instrument for their savings and the reasons for your recommendation.

Emyli is 20 years old, gets paid weekly, and wants to start saving (but with her bills it will not be much). She is just starting out in her apartment so unexpected expenditures may occur that will necessitate her dipping into her savings.

Julie is 55 years old, has $60,000 to invest, and a six figure annual income. She has good health and disability insurance at her job and an emergency fund equal to eight months' expenses. She wishes to reduce her tax liability and is not adverse to taking a chance. She has a good pension plan and other savings.

Chan is 35 years old, has some discretionary income each paycheck and about $800 in savings. He may wish to buy a car in 12 to 18 months with this money. The safety of his investment is of primary importance to him.

Juan is 45 years old and has about $35,000 to invest. Taxes are an issue as his income is high and his deductions low. He wishes to get a good return but is a poor financial planner so may need to dip into his savings from time to time.

3. The following is a summary of information from your July bank statement and checkbook.

Bank statement data:

Balance 7-31-96	$286.50		
Checks cleared:		Deposits:	
#906	$18.00	7-15	$214.00
910	26.00		
912	9.00	Interest for July	$2.37
913	120.00		
915	47.00	EFT charge to transfer money from out-of-town	$10

Your checkbook shows:

Balance 7-31-96	$309.13		
Checks written:		Deposits:	
#910	$26.00	7-15	$214.00
911	35.00	7-31	196.00
912	90.00		
913	120.00	June interest	$3.14
914	51.00		
915	47.00		

Your June bank reconciliation showed two outstanding checks: #906 for $18.00 and #909 for $14.00.

a. Prepare your July bank reconciliation.

b. Based on your reconciliation, what will you need to record in your checkbook?

4. Contact at least three financial institutions and gather the information needed to complete the worksheet "Choosing a Financial Institution." Be sure to consider Other Issues that you may wish to ask about (hours of operation, how interest is compounded). After you have gathered the information answer the following questions.

a. Reviewing the list of criteria, what are the five most important to your banking needs?

1.

2.

3.

4.

5.

b. Based on the five criteria most important to you, which financial institution would you select? Briefly explain your answer.

Chapter 4 Solutions

What Do You Know?

1.	F	6.	T
2.	F	7.	F
3.	T	8.	F
4.	T	9.	F
5.	T	10.	F

Key Terminology Exercise - Matching

1.	L	9.	G
2.	R	10.	M
3.	A	11.	J
4.	C	12.	F
5.	H	13.	T
6.	O	14.	K
7.	B	15.	Q
8.	S		

Multiple Choice Questions

1.	c	10.	b
2.	d	11.	d
3.	b	12.	b
4.	d	13.	d
5.	c	14.	d
6.	a	15.	c
7.	b	16.	c
8.	b	17.	c
9.	d	18.	c

Experiential Problems

1.

Exhibit 4.6

Comparing the Major Savings Options

Instrument / Criteria	Statement Savings and NOW Accounts	Bank CDs	U.S. Treasury Issues	Money Market Mutual Funds	Bank Money Market Accounts
Minimum Investment	Varies from bank to bank.	Varies from bank to bank.			Varies from bank to bank.
Liquidity	Can withdraw money without penalty.	Specified maturities.	Specified maturities.	Can withdraw money without penalty.	
Yield	Rates set at bank's discretion.	Rates set at bank's discretion.		Vary with market interest rates.	Set at bank's discretion. Vary with market interest rates.
Safety	Federally insured up to $100,000.	Federally insured up to $100,000.			
Taxation	Interest is taxable at federal state and local levels.	Interest is taxable at federal state and local levels.			Interest is taxable at federal state and local levels.
Summary	Safe. Convenient to get at.	Safe. Flexible in choice of maturities. Convenient to get at.	Safe. Flexible in choice of maturities.	Generally safe. Easy access to funds.	

2. Emyli - Statement Savings and NOW accounts.

> Reasons - low or no minimum
> can withdraw without penalty
> insured

Julie - U.S. Treasury Issues or Money Market Mutual Funds

> Reasons - has enough money to use these
> tax advantages - with right mutual fund
> good return

Chan - Bank CD

> Reasons - low minimum investment
> flexible in choice of maturities
> insured

Juan - Money Market Mutual Funds

> Reasons - has the required minimum
> possible tax advantages
> can withdraw without penalty
> no limit on withdrawals unlike bank money market accounts

Note: Your answers and/or reasons may vary from these. It does not mean that your responses are not valid. Discuss your answers and/or reasons that differ with your instructor. Personal values may influence your response.

3. a. There are two formats to use in reconciling a checkbook. Both will get the job done and are presented here for your convenience. Use whichever you prefer.

Format 1		Format 2	
Balance per bank statement	$286.50	Balance per bank	$286.50
Deposit not shown by bank (in transit)	+196.00	Deposit not shown by bank (in transit)	+196.00
Outstanding checks:		Outstanding checks:	
#909 (June) $14.00		#909 (June) $14.00	
911 35.00		911 35.00	
914 51.00	-100.00	914 51.00	-100.00
July interest	-2.37	Available cash	$382.50
EFT charge	+10.00		
Error on check #912	-81.00	Balance per checkbook	$309.13
Balance per checkbook	$309.13	July interest	+2.87
		EFT charge	-10.00
		Error on check #912	+81.00
		Available cash	$382.50

b. July interest - add $2.37 to balance in checkbook
   EFT charge - subtract $10.00 from balance in checkbook

Chapter 5

Credit Management

What Do You Know?

T F 1. My current debt is no more than 20% of my annual after-tax income, excluding mortgage.

T F 2. I use credit cards for convenience, not because I don't have the money to pay for purchases.

T F 3. My credit cards have no annual fees.

T F 4. I know the APR for my credit cards.

T F 5. I reviewed a copy of my credit report recently.

T F 6. I have credit established in my own name.

T F 7. I have never filed bankruptcy.

T F 8. I have never had my wages garnished.

T F 9. I have never defaulted on a loan.

T F 10. I know I cannot be denied credit because of my age or marital status.

Chapter 5

Credit Management

Chapter Overview

Credit has become part of the American way of life. There are right, as well as wrong, reasons for borrowing. In addition, there are right, as well as wrong, sources from which you may borrow. Comparision shopping for credit is just as important as comparison shopping for a new car. While credit is used as a convenience for many of us, for others, credit is an abuse. It is important to know the symptoms of credit abuse. Help exists for those who know where and when to get it.

Chapter Outline

I.   What Is Credit

    A.   Types of consumer credit

        1.   definition - loan plus interest on a regular basis for a specified time period

        2.   revolving (open-end) charge accounts - purchases as often as wanted up to a certain limit

        3.   closed-end installment purchase plans - written agreement for each purchase

        4.   regular (30-day) charge accounts - repay in full in 30 days

        5.   mortgage loans

    B.   Deciding how much to borrow - no more than 10-20% take-home pay

    C.   The right reasons for borrowing

        1.   purchasing large, important goods and services

        2.   dealing with emergencies

        3.   taking advantage of opportunities

        4.   convenience

        5.   establishing or improving credit rating

    D.   The wrong reasons for borrowing

        1.   to meet basic living expenses

        2.   to make impulse purchases

        3.   to purchase short-lived goods and services

II. Sources of Consumer Credit

    A. Financial institutions

    B. National credit cards

    C. Credit cards issued by retailers

    D. Consumer finance companies

    E. Life insurance companies

    F. Brokerage account loans

    G. Personal loans from family/friends

    H. Pawnbrokers

III. Applying For Credit

    A. What creditors look for

        1. capacity

        2. character

        3. collateral

    B. The role of credit bureaus

    C. What to do if you're denied credit

    D. Legislation governing consumer credit

IV. The Cost of Borrowing

    A. Calculating Total Finance Charges

        1. finance charge

        2. APR

        3. principal

        4. $ amount borrowed x APR x loan term = finance charges

    B. Calculating periodic interest on loans

        1. simple interest

        2. fully amortized

    C. Choosing the lowest cost credit card

        1. annual fee

        2. APR

        3. length of grace period

V. Credit Abuse

    A. Repossession

    B. Wage garnishment

    C. Bankruptcy

    D. Are you developing a problem with credit?

    C. Credit counseling

Name _____   Instructor _____

Date _____   Section _____

Key Terminology Exercise - Fill In

Using the terms from the Running Glossary in your text, complete the following statements.

1. The difference between the total dollars paid back and the _____ is called the _____.

2. Your car may be subject to _____ if you _____ on the loan by missing payments.

3. Anytime you pay later for a purchase you are using a form of _____.

4. VISA and Master Card are _____, which limit your total purchases to a specified amount.

5. When you purchase a home with a mortgage, the house is the _____ for the loan.

6. Some credit cards give you a _____ of 25 to 30 days to pay your balance before any interest is charged.

7. A lender will measure your ability to repay a loan by your _____ and your willingness to repay by your _____.

8. Before you use _____ to eliminate your credit problems you should see a _____ who may be able to work out a repayment schedule.

9. Phil Rizzuto does TV ads for The Money Store which is an example of a(n) _____.

10. A car loan where the monthly payments result in your owing nothing at the end of the loan period is a(n) _____.

Name _____   Instructor _____

Date _____   Section _____

Multiple Choice Questions

1. All of the following are generally purchased on credit **except**
   a. homes.
   b. cars.
   c. utilities (gas, electric, telephone).
   d. a and b, only
   e. a, b and c

2. Revolving (open-end) charge accounts do **not** include
   a. specified credit limit.
   b. monthly statement of transactions.
   c. fixed monthly payment.
   d. a and b, only
   e. b and c, only

3. Closed-end installment purchase plans require a written agreement that specifies
   a. the total finance charges.
   b. the amount to be paid each installment.
   c. the length of the repayment period.
   d. all of the above
   e. a and c, only

4. The percentage of your take-home that is used to repay installment debt should not exceed
   a. 5% to 10%
   b. 10% to 20%
   c. 15% to 30%
   d. 35% to 40%
   e. 50% to 60%

5. All of the following are good reasons to use credit **except**
   a. to purchase large, important goods and services.
   b. to purchase items to be paid for from future raises.
   c. dealing with emergencies.
   d. taking advantage of opportunities.
   e. to avoid carrying large amounts of cash.

Harcourt Brace & Company

6. A sign that you are using credit to live beyond you means is
    a. using credit to pay basic living expenses.
    b. using credit for impulse purchases.
    c. using credit to purchase short-lived goods.
    d. all of the above
    e. a and c, only

7. If you made a $4,000 purchase on an 18% credit card and made the minimum monthly payment of 2.5% of the outstanding balance or $25 (whichever is higher), your total interest paid would be approximately
    a. over $4,000.
    b. $3,000.
    c. $2,000.
    d. $1,000.
    e. $500.

8. In question #7, how long would it take you to pay off your purchase?
    a. less than 2 years
    b. 2 to 5 years
    c. 5 to 10 years
    d. 10 to 15 years
    e. over 15 years

9. VISA and Master Card can only be obtained from
    a. financial institutions.
    b. airlines.
    c. oil companies.
    d. all of the above
    e. a and c, only

10. All of the following apply to consumer finance companies **except**
    a. they make loans as small as $100.
    b. they make unsecured loans.
    c. they charge about the same interest as a bank.
    d. their maximum loan is set by state law.
    e. they may be easier to deal with than a bank.

11. The advantage to borrowing from relatives is
    a. you can get better interest rates than at a bank.
    b. relatives are less likely to repo your car.
    c. you need not be business-like.
    d. a and b, only
    e. a, b and c

12. In order to obtain credit you must
    a. have the capacity to repay the loan.
    b. have demonstrated a willingness to pay your debits.
    c. something of value to secure the loan (this may be your good name).
    d. a and c, only
    e. a, b and c

13. To establish a good credit history on which to secure first time credit
    a. have a telephone billed in your name.
    b. apply for oil-company credit cards, but do not use them.
    c. open a checking and savings account.
    d. a and c, only
    e. a, b and c

14. Federal laws require that
    a. all finance charges be disclosed on a loan.
    b. your liability is limited to $50 on a lost credit card.
    c. you can withold payment and not be charged interest on a credit card purchase you deem unsatisfactory in quality.
    d. you cannot be denied credit soley on the basis of age.
    e. all of the above

15. The total finance charges will be determined by all of the following **except**
    a. the item purchased.
    b. amount of the purchase.
    c. the interest rate.
    d. the number of monthly payments.
    e. all of the above

16. When interest on a loan is calculated using the simple interest method the amount of interest in each monthly payment will
    a. increase each month.
    b. stay the same.
    c. decrease each month.
    d. not enough information given to tell.
    e. vary each month, up or down.

17. The grace period on a credit card will
    a. decrease the interest you pay.
    b. have no effect on the interest you pay.
    c. increase the interest you pay.
    d. allow you to pay no interest if you pay the balance in the grace period.
    e. have some effect depending on the terms.

18. If a person has no hope of repaying their debts they should file bankruptcy under
    a. Chapter 7.
    b. Chapter 9.
    c. Chapter 11.
    d. Chapter 13.
    e. all of the above

19. If you get into credit trouble you should do all of the following **except**
    a. get your records in order.
    b. establish a realistic budget.
    c. keep only one credit card with a low limit.
    d. forgo any attempt at saving.
    e. seek credit counseling.

Name _____   Instructor _____

Date _____   Section _____

Experiential Problems

1. You have your eye on a home entertainment package at a local store that regularly sells for $3,500 and has all the extras that you desire. In today's local paper you see the store has your package on sale for $3,000. The sale is only for the next month and, based on past experience, may not be repeated.

   After giving the matter serious consideration you have identified the following three options.

   Option #1. You have $3,000 in your emergency fund, a money market mutual fund currently yielding 6%.

   Option #2. Your VISA card has $3,000 available credit. The interest rate is 18% and your card has a 30 day grace period.

   Option #3. You can put money into your money market mutual fund each month until you have saved enough. This will mean forgoing the sale and paying the full price of $3,500.

   Your budget will allow you to spend $150 per month on this project. For simplicity ignore sales taxes in your calculations and assume the first $150 payment is made in 30 days.

   a. Compute the monetary cost of each of the options. (Hint: Consider opportunity cost where appropriate. Refer to Exhibit 5.7 in your text for option #2). Based on the monetary cost, which option would you choose?

Option #1   Option #2   Option #3

b. List the non-monetary cost of each option.

c. Considering both the monetary and non-monetary aspects of the three options, which would you choose and why?

2. For your own protection you should review a copy of your credit report annually. This will alert you to any errors or unauthorized use of your name for credit purposes. TRW will give you one free report each year. To get your free copy call 800-682-7654. When it arrives review it carefully. If you need assistance ask your professor or a loan officer at a bank if you know one.

3. Complete the following worksheet to compute the percentage of your take-home pay that goes to pay installment debt.

   a. Is the percentage within the recommended limits of 10% to 20%?

   b. Compare the reasons for the loans to the values and goals you identified in chapter 1. Do you see any loans that do not seem consistent with your values and goals? If yes, write a brief analysis as to the reason for that inconsistency. Should your goals be revised?

Worksheet
Summary of Outstanding Loans

Type of Loan	Original Amount	Current Balance	Months Left	Annual Percentage Rate	Monthly Payment
Personal Loans					
1. _____					
2. _____					
Automobile Loans					
1. _____					
2. _____					
Credit Cards					
1. _____					
2. _____					
3. _____					
4. _____					
Other Loans or Debts					
1. _____					
2. _____					
3. _____					
4. _____					

Total Monthly Payments = _____

Monthly Take-Home Pay:_____ x .20 = _____

x .15 = _____

x .10 = _____

4. Make a list of all of your credit cards - VISA, Master Card, oil company, department store, etc. - that includes the following information:

    1. name of issuer
    2. account number
    3. interest rate
    4. credit limit
    5. 800 number to call if lost

    a. Once your list is complete, add up the total of the credit limit for all the cards. Ask yourself if you need this much available credit. Remember that the total credit available, even unused, may impact the decision of a future lender. If the answer to the question you ask yourself above is ''No'' consider closing some of the accounts.

    b. When or if you have eliminated some of the accounts on your list, place the list in a safe place. If you ever lose your wallet/purse this ready list of 800 numbers will prove most useful. Be sure to update the list when appropriate.

Chapter 5 Solutions

What Do You Know?

1. T
2. T
3. T
4. T
5. T
6. T
7. T
8. T
9. T
10. T

Key Terminology Exercise - Fill In

1. principle, finance charges
2. repossession, default
3. credit
4. revolving charge accounts
5. collateral
6. grace period
7. capacity for credit, character
8. bankruptcy, credit counselor
9. consumer finance company
10. fully amortized loan

Multiple Choice Questions

1. e
2. c
3. d
4. b
5. b
6. d
7. a
8. e
9. d
10. c
11. d
12. e
13. d
14. e
15. a
16. c
17. d
18. a
19. d

Experiential Problems

1. a. The cost is the opportunity cost minus lost interest. You rebuild the fund by making $150 deposits monthly until the $3,000 is replaced.

Option #1

End of Month	Balance	Lost interest for month
1	$-3,000.00	$15.00 ($3000 x 6%/12)
2	-2,850.00	14.25 (2850 x 6%/12)
3	-2,700.00	13.50
4	-2,550.00	12.75
5	-2,400.00	12.00
6	-2,250.00	11.25
7	-2,100.00	10.50
8	-1,950.00	9.75
9	-1,800.00	9.00
10	-1,650.00	8.25
11	-1,500.00	7.50
12	-1,350.00	6.75
13	-1,200.00	6.00
14	-1,050.00	5.25
15	-900.00	4.50
16	-750.00	3.75
17	-600.00	3.00
18	-450.00	2.22
19	-300.00	1.50
20	-150.00	.75
	Total cost	$157.50 lost interest
		(opportunity cost)

Option #2

Month	Beginning Balance	Interest	Payment	Principal Repaid	Ending Balance
1	$3,000.00	(Grace period)	$150.00	$150.00	$2,850.00
2	2,850.00	42.75		107.25	2,742.75
3	2,742.75	41.14		108.86	2,633.89
4	2,633.89	39.50		110.50	2,523.39
5	2,523.39	37.85		112.15	2,411.24
6	2,411.24	36.17		113.83	2,297.41
7	2,297.41	34.46		115.54	2,181.97
8	2,181.87	32.73		117.27	2,064.60
9	2,064.60	30.97		119.03	1,945.57
10	1,945.57	29.18		120.82	1,824.75
11	1,824.75	27.37		122.63	1,702.12
12	1,702.12	25.53		124.47	1,577.65
13	1,577.65	23.66		126.34	1,451.31
14	1,451.31	21.77		128.23	1,323.08
15	1,323.08	19.85		130.15	1,192.93
16	1,192.93	17.89		132.11	1,060.82
17	1,060.82	15.91		134.09	926.73
18	926.73	13.90		136.10	790.63
19	790.63	11.86		138.14	652.49
20	652.49	9.79		140.12	512.28
21	512.28	7.68		142.32	369.96
22	369.96	5.55		144.45	225.51
23	225.51	3.38		146.62	78.89
24	78.89	1.18	80.07	78.89	0
	Total Cost	$530.07	finance charges		

Option #3

Month	Deposit	(including Interest) Balance*
1	$150.00	$150.00
2	150.00	300.75
3	150.00	452.25
4	150.00	604.51
5	150.00	757.53
6	150.00	911.32
7	150.00	1,065.88
8	150.00	1,221.21
9	150.00	1,377.32
10	150.00	1,534.21
11	150.00	1,691.88
12	150.00	1,850.34
13	150.00	2,009.59
14	150.00	2,169.64
15	150.00	2,330.48
16	150.00	2,492.13
17	150.00	2,654.59
18	150.00	2,817.86
19	150.00	2,981.95
20	150.00	3,146.86
21	150.00	3,312.59
22	150.00	3,479.15
23	150.00	3,496.54
24	150.00	3,528.34
	0.00	

*   To compute the balance use the following formula. Previous month balance + (Previous month balance x .06/12) + current month's deposit.

The cost of this option is the lost savings less the interest earned on the account

Lost savings	$500.00
Interest earned**	228.34
Total cost	$271.66

** Balance in fund end of 24th month $3,528.34
     Total deposited ($150 x 23)   3,300.00
     Interest Earned $228.34

(Note - the interest would be taxable depending on your personal tax situation. We have ignored the tax impact in our calculations - but it would increase the cost of option #3 somewhat.)

Conclusion:

Based solely on the monetary cost, the three options rank as follows:

Option #1 $157.50
Option #3 $271.66
Option #2 $530.07

b.   Option #1- you will be without your emergency fund if you need it.

Option #2- you will not have the credit available if you need it.

Option #3- you will not have the entertainment package for two years.

c.   This is a personal choice that will vary from student to student. If not having the emergency fund available will cause you to lose sleep, you may choose option #2 or #3. If you must have the package now and cannot wait, only option #1 and #2 are viable.

Chapter 6

Understanding Taxes

What Do You Know?

T F 1. An increase on the tax on liquor is designed to discourage drinking.

T F 2. I can name 5 different types of taxes levied by the government.

T F 3. Having extra tax money withheld from your paycheck is a smart way to save money.

T F 4. If I receive money as a gift, I have to pay taxes on it as it is just like income.

T F 5. My employer and I split the Social Security and medicare taxes I owe each year.

T F 6. Depending on where you live, your taxes could vary by several thousand dollars.

T F 7. I believe people should fear, or at least be nervous, about the IRS.

T F 8. Typically, my family/I file for a tax extension.

T F 9. The IRS catches people who mistakenly pay too much in taxes.

T F 10. If the IRS calls you in for an audit, you may send someone in your place.

Chapter 6

Understanding Taxes

Chapter Overview

As the old saying goes, "there are only two things in life that are certain: death and taxes." However, after Tax Freedom Day - May 7 - you only have to worry about death, at least until next year. On average, Americans must work from January 1 through May 7 to pay their taxes. Therefore it is wise to understand the different types of taxes as well as when and how to acquire professional tax advice.

Chapter Outline

I. What Are Taxes

    A. Philosophies of taxation

        1. benefits - received philosophy

        2. ability to pay philosophy

    B. Tax impact on households

        1. progressive tax

        2. regressive tax

    C. Tax rates

        1. average or effective

        2. marginal

II. Types Of Taxes

    A. Federal income tax

    B. State and local income tax

    C. Social Security and Medicare taxes

    D. Property taxes

    E. Sales taxes

    F. Excise taxes

    G. State and local licensing fees

    H. How much people pay in taxes

III. The Federal Income Tax System

   A. How the IRS works

   B. Taxpayer compliance

      1. tax audit

      2. correspondence audit

   C. Dealing with the IRS

      1. have written documentation

      2. never give more information than asked

      3. have a tax professional present

      4. don't agree for the sake of agreeing

   D. Proposed changes to the federal tax system

IV. Preparing Your Federal Tax Return

   A. Completing your tax forms

   B. Filing your tax return

V. Getting Help With Your Taxes

   A. Who doesn't need a tax professional

      1. earn less than $50,000

      2. no outside income other than interest or dividends

      3. few unusual deductions

      4. no complicated investments or life situations

   B. Help from the IRS

      1. toll-free IRS telephone

      2. visit local IRS office

      3. mail-in questions

      4. Internet

      5. goal is to <u>assist</u> you

   C. Using a tax preparation firm

      1. speed

      2. convenience

      3. inexpensive

      4. serious limitations

    D. Using a tax accountant if you

        1. sold or bought property

        2. own rental property

        3. pay quarterly estimated taxes

        4. deduct home as an office

        5. use car for business

        6. are involved in a divorce

        7. earn a high income

    E. Tax information sources

VI. Tax Planning

    A. Tax evasion vs. tax avoidance

    B. Tax-saving tips

Name _____   Instructor _____

Date _____   Section _____

Key Terminology Exercise - Crossword Puzzle

Using the terms in the Running Glossary, complete the crossword puzzle. An x indicates a space in a multi-word answer.

Across

3. Type of tax where the tax rate increases as income increases.
6. What you never want from the IRS is a(n) _____.
7. This is a goal of tax planning.
8. Income, sales, excise, tolls are examples of a(n) _____.
9. The tax rate of the top tax bracket that you are in.
10. The interest on your home mortgages is a tax-_____.

Down

1. An item deducted directly from your tax bill is a tax _____.
2. When Al Capone failed to pay his taxes he went to prison for tax-_____.
4. A tax that hits the poor harder than the rich.
5. The percentage of your income paid in taxes is determined by this.

Name _____   Instructor _____

Date _____   Section _____

Multiple Choice Questions

1. If you wish to avoid paying both a state income tax and a state sales tax, you will need to move to
    a. Maine.
    b. Hawaii.
    c. New Hampshire.
    d. North Dakota.

2. According to a recent survey, in regards to the basics of taxes and tax planning Americans knew?
    a. less than half of the information on the survey
    b. more than half of the information on the survey
    c. almost nothing of the information on the survey
    d. almost everything of the information of the survey

3. Because of the recent changes in the tax codes, careful tax planning today is
    a. useless.
    b. somewhat important.
    c. slightly important.
    d. essential.

4. Taxes are collected for all of the following **except**
    a. day to day expenses of running a government.
    b. regulating people's habits and behavior.
    c. controlling the economy.
    d. all of the above

5. Which of the following is a tax based on the benefits-received philosophy?
    a. property taxes
    b. income taxes
    c. tolls on bridges
    d. sales taxes

6. Ability to pay philosophy is the basis for
    a. progressive tax.
    b. regressive tax.
    c. aggressive tax.
    d. all of the above

7. Last year you earned $50,000 and paid 20% of your income in taxes. This year you got a $5,000 raise but your tax bill went up by $1,500, more than 20% of your raise. This was the result of
   a. average tax rate.
   b. marginal tax rate.
   c. sur tax rate.
   d. premium tax rate.

8. Income taxes may be levied by all of the following except
   a. federal governments.
   b. state governments.
   c. county governments.
   d. all of the above

9. The greatest amount of tax dollars Americans pay are collected through
   a. sales taxes.
   b. social security taxes.
   c. federal income taxes.
   d. property taxes.

10. Gasoline taxes on the state level
    a. vary only slightly from state to state.
    b. vary greatly from state to state.
    c. vary not at all from state to state.
    d. do not exist as only the federal government taxes gasoline.

11. The Internal Revenue Service is a branch of the
    a. Justice Department.
    b. Congress.
    c. U.S. Treasury Department.
    d. Executive Branch.

12. If you fail to pay the taxes for which you are legally liable, you will be required to pay
    a. additional tax assessments.
    b. interest charges.
    c. penalties.
    d. all of the above

13. Of the tax returns it receives each year the IRS audits
    a. less than 1%.
    b. about 5%.
    c. over 10%.
    d. over 15%.

14. When dealing with the IRS in an audit you should
    a. volunteer as much information as possible.
    b. pay what they tell you is due; they do not negotiate.
    c. sign what they tell you to; you can always appeal.
    d. ask for their installment plan to pay what you owe.

15. The proposed "flat tax" would result in
    a. lower taxes for all.
    b. higher taxes for all.
    c. lower taxes for the rich.
    d. higher taxes for the rich.

16. Which of the following people should seek the services of a professional tax preparer?
    a. someone who earns $85,000 a year
    b. someone who has business investments in Poland and Bolivia
    c. someone who supports their parents in a nursing home and has a physically challenged child
    d. they all need a professional

17. All of the following can represent you before the IRS in a tax audit **except**
    a. a tax attorney.
    b. a CPA.
    c. an enrolled agent.
    d. a tax preparation company.

18. Getting paid in cash for a job to avoid paying taxes on the income is
    a. tax avoidance.
    b. tax evasion.
    c. tax deferring.
    d. tax planning.

19. Investing in bonds, the interest on which is not taxable, is an example of
    a. tax avoidance.
    b. tax evasion.
    c. tax deferring.
    d. tax accruing.

Harcourt Brace & Company

Name _____   Instructor _____

Date _____   Section _____

Experiential Problems

1. Referring to the tax-savings tips on page 188 in the text, indicate which of the following expenses are deductible (D), not deductible (ND), maybe deductible, depending upon income (?).

    _____ A. interest paid on a home equity loan taken out to finance a vacation home

    _____ B. interest paid on a home equity loan taken out to fiance a down payment on a new car

    _____ C. billings for 45 visits to a psychologist for 45 hours of therapy at $85.00 per hour

    _____ D. theft of 5 cd's and some clothes from your automobile

    _____ E. faculty dues to the Association of Collegiate Business Schools and Programs

    _____ F. suits, high heels, and hosiery for a office job

    _____ G. lab coats for a medical job

    _____ H. subscription to a magazine for accountants and I'm working on a degree in accounting

    _____ I. subscription to a magazine for accountants and I'm a working accountant

    _____ J. the amount paid to Joe Smadlap C.P.A. to do my taxes

2. For the people listed below determine who if anybody they should see as a tax preparer/advisor.

   a. Frank is 52 years old, earns $150,000 as a doctor, and is in a professional corporation with four other doctors. He also has part interest in an Austrian horse farm, a Canadian ski lodge and a small shopping center in Fargo. All of these enterprises are making money.

   b. Ed is 19 years old and earns $12,000 delivering pizza while he attends college. He has 10 shares of Disney Studios in his portfolio.

   c. Nancy is 36 years old, earns $60,000 as a bulldozer operator, and is divorced with two children. She receives child support, alimony and income from a trust fund her dad left to her.

   d. Myrtle and Stanley are 40 and 41 years old with combined income of $48,000. They have one son in college and one in the army. They own a house and have some stocks and bonds. Stanley works part time at a local pub bartending.

3. Conduct informational interviews with 3 professionals from the following list:

   ___ enrolled agent

   ___ CPA tax specialist

   ___ tax preparation company

   ___ tax attorney

   ___ independent local tax preparation service

Informational interviews are explained in detail on page 2-10 to 2-12. Specific questions for these interviews are found on page 197 ("Advice from the Experts") in the text. Here are some additional questions.

*Describe your typical customer.

*As a tax specialist, what do you do best?

*Which customer needs do you refer out? To where? (Not company name but occupational title.)

*How many customers have you represented before the IRS in tax audits?

*How creative are you with regards to tax planning?

Chapter 6 Solutions

What Do You Know?

1. T
2. T
3. F
4. F
5. T

6. T
7. F
8. F
9. T
10. T

Key Terminology Exercise - Crossword Puzzle

Across

1. credits
2. evasion
4. regressive tax
5. average tax rate

Down

3. progressive tax
6. audit
7. avoidance
8. tax
9. marginal tax rate
10. deductions

Multiple Choice Questions

1. c
2. a
3. d
4. d
5. c
6. a
7. b
8. d
9. c
10. b

11. c
12. d
13. a
14. d
15. c
16. d
17. d
18. b
19. a

Experiential Problems

1.

A. D
B. D
C. ?
D. ?

E. ?
F. ND
G. ?
H. ND

I. ?
J. ?

2. This is a judgement call so your answers may differ from the ones below.

   a. Frank has an international and complex tax situation. At his age and income he needs tax planning help. A tax attorney is advisable.

   b. Ed should buy a simple book at his local bookstore and do his own. He cannot afford nor does he need professional help.

   c. Nancy's situation is complex enough for professional help but not enough for a tax attorney. Tax planning is called for, so a CPA is probably her best choice. Her income is enough to comfortably afford this kind of help.

   d. Myrtle and Stanley could probably do their own with some study, but will probably find a tax preparation company or a local tax service more to their liking.

Part 3

Effective Buying

Chapter 7

Transportation and Other Major Consumer Decisions

What Do You Know?

T F 1. I consider my car an investment.

T F 2. I believe extended service warranties are good to have.

T F 3. The "protection" package for new cars of rustproofing, paint sealants, and fabric protection may be marked up as high as 1,000%.

T F 4. Depreciation is the most expensive part of owning a car.

T F 5. I understand the difference between my needs and wants.

T F 6. If 2 cars cost the same, I could save money by researching information and buying the car which depreciates less.

T F 7. My purchasing decisions are influenced by my personality and pervious experience.

T F 8. My car was financed for more than 3 years.

T F 9. When leasing a car, at the end of the lease period, you own the car.

T F 10. Leasing a car is always cheaper than buying.

Chapter 7

Transportation and Other Major Consumer Decisions

Chapter Overview

"Can I really afford this?" is a question most of us ask ourselves many times. Though we all go through some sort of decision-making process, the best way to get the most for our money is to follow a planned, step-by-step approach. Recognition of the difference between our needs and our wants is an important step. Making informed decisions is another valuable part of the process. Cars represent the largest purchase you will make, after a home and a college education. Researching the purchase as well as the financing may save you hundreds if not thousands of dollars.

Chapter Outline

I. How Consumers Make Purchase Decisions

    A. A model of consumer decision making

        1. depends on

            a. what the purchase is

            b. how important it is

            c. how often you buy it

            d. how the purchase will affect your finances

        2. step-by-step approach

            a. goals

            b. define the opportunity or situation

            c. evaluation of alternatives

            d. purchase decision

            e. purchase act

            f. post purchase evaluation

        3. benefits

            a. take advantage of sales, bargains, and unplanned opportunities

            b. planning allows for added convenience and least expensive payment method

            c. avoid impulse buying, unneeded items, and purchasing mistakes

    B. Separating needs from wants

    C. Fitting a major expenditure into your budget

II. Your Rights as a Consumer

  A. Consumer fraud and abuse

    1. mail and phone frauds

    2. home and auto repairs

    3. deceptive advertising

    4. deceptive sales practices and pricing

  B. Sources of consumer assistance

    1. <u>Consumer's Resource Handbook</u>

    2. Better Business Bureau

    3. Consumers Union

    4. Underwriters Laboratories (UL)

    5. using the media

    6. selected federal agencies

    7. state and local consumer protection services

  C. How to complain and get action

    1. decide what the problem is and what remedy you are requesting

    2. contact the salesperson

    3. write a letter to the company

    4. take 3rd party action

III. The Transportation Decision

  A. Do you need a car?

    1. 3rd largest monetary purchase after house, and a college education

    2. average new car = $20,000

    3. average used car = $10,000

    4. 4 out of 5 miles are driven because of work or family

    5. transportation alternatives limited in small cities and rural areas

    6. cost and scarcity of parking in large cities is a problem

    7. public transportation in large cities may be faster than driving

    8. consider:

      a. walking

      b. biking

      c. public transportation

      d. car-pooling

B. The cost of owning and operating a car

   1. cars are not an investment; they depreciate over time (60% in 5 years)

   2. costs include

      a. depreciation

      b. financing

      c. insurance

      d. routine maintenance

      e. repairs

      f. registration

      g. gas

   3. average new car costs 46 cents a mile to own and operate

IV. How to Purchase an Automobile

A. Choosing the right car for you

   1. make and model

   2. size

   3. body style

   4. options

   5. cost of ownership

B. A new car or a used car

   1. used car benefits

      a. less expensive to buy

      b. depreciates less

      c. increased quality

      d. transferable warranties as a second owner

      e. most desirable are:

        1) less than 4 years old

        2) 15,000-25,000 miles

        3) models with "quality" reputation

   2. used car sources

      a. about half through private deals

      b. new car dealers

      c. used car dealers

      d. NADA Used Car Guide

C. Choosing a new car dealer and closing the sale

   1. sticker price

   2. negotiating

      3. extra costs

      4. alternatives to negotiations

      5. trade-in

   D. Warranties

      1. bumper-to-bumper

      2. power-trail

V. Financing The Car Purchase

   A. Sources of financing

      1. banks

      2. credit unions

      3. auto manufacturer finance subsidiary

   B. Evaluating ''low-rate'' financing incentives

   C. The leasing alternative

      1. negotiate the price

      2. know the rate used to compute lease payment

      3. know the advantages and disadvantages of a high residual value of the car

      4. determine whether the mileage limit is fair

      5. check the warranty so it covers the entire lease period

      6. understand the ''excess wear and tear'' clause

Name _____   Instructor _____

Date _____   Section _____

Key Terminology Exercise - Crossword Puzzle

Using the terms in the Running Glossary, complete the crossword puzzle. An X indicates a space in a multi-word answer.

<u>Across</u>

2. In this court you serve as your own attorney.

5. A mansion with servants, pool and tennis courts is this.

6. A roof over your head is this.

7. Start negotiating at this price for your car.

<u>Down</u>

1. Use this to get your new car repaired if something goes wrong.

3. When you go from store to store to see who has the lowest price you are doing this kind of shopping.

4. Never pay this price for a car.

Name _____ Instructor _____

Date _____ Section _____

Multiple Choice Questions

1. The largest single cost of owning and operating a car is
   a. gasoline.
   b. repairs.
   c. depreciation.
   d. insurance.

2. Extended service warranties on new cars are
   a. an absolute necessity.
   b. rarely worth what they cost.
   c. O.K. but not always necessary.
   d. not usually available.

3. "Paks" such as rustproofing, paint sealants and fabric protection are
   a. are sometimes marked up 1,000%.
   b. are unnecessary on today's cars.
   c. may be harmful to the car.
   d. all of the above

4. In the process of making a major purchase you would
   a. consult family, friends and acquaintances.
   b. look at advertisements.
   c. talk to sales representatives.
   d. consider your attitudes and personality.
   e. all of the above

5. In order to make the best and most beneficial decisions you should **not**
   a. keep informed.
   b. budget carefully.
   c. change decisions on advice of salespeople.
   d. rush your decisions.

6. Which of the following is most likely a want rather than a need?
   a. a house
   b. a Cadillac
   c. a Big Mac
   d. an education

7. To protect yourself from consumer fraud and abuse you should
   a. make a good decision; it's all you need to do.
   b. have a guarantee.
   c. know the sources of consumer assistance.
   d. all of the above

8. The areas where consumers need **not** be concerned about fraud and consumer abuse is
   a. auto repairs.
   b. food purchases.
   c. mail order purchases.
   d. all are troublesome areas

9. All of the following are government agencies or departments to which a consumer can turn for assistance **except**
   a. state attorney general.
   b. Federal Trade Commission.
   c. Better Business Bureau.
   d. Food and Drug Administration.

10. Possibly the quickest and simplest way to get a problem with a business resolved is to
    a. sue them is small claims court.
    b. call the consumer action line on the evening TV news.
    c. contact the Better Business Bureau.
    d. file an action before the Federal Trade Commission.

11. To deal with a complaint you should
    a. decide what is the problem.
    b. contact the person who sold you the product.
    c. ask them what they can do to solve the problem.
    d. a and b, only

12. To utilize small claims court you need **not**
    a. limit your claims as small claims court handles amounts under (typically $1,000) some dollar figure.
    b. hire an attorney.
    c. pay a small filing fee.
    d. give up your right to appeal if you lose.

13. What is the percentage of miles driven by passenger cars in the U.S. that is considered nonessential?
    a. 20%
    b. 40%
    c. 50%
    d. 70%

14. After five years cars will lose about what percent of their original cost?
    a. 40%   c. 80%
    b. 20%   d. 60%

15. Which of the following is not an issue you should consider in buying a car?
    a. make and model
    b. options
    c. dealership
    d. all of the above

16. Foreign cars come with
    a. more available options than American cars.
    b. fewer available options than American cars.
    c. about the same available options than American cars.
    d. have few, if any, options.

17. The major difference in operating costs of similarly priced cars is
    a. insurance.
    b. repairs.
    c. depreciation.
    d. gas mileage.

18. Used cars are gaining in popularity because
    a. cost of new cars.
    b. increased quality.
    c. transferable warranties.
    d. all of the above

19. Of the extra costs a car dealer may spring on you, which of the following is really fair for you to pay?
    a. extended warranties
    b. fees to prepare paper work
    c. rust-proofing, paint sealant and fabric protection
    d. all of the above

20. The cheapest source of auto financing can usually be obtained from
    a. commercial banks.
    b. credit unions.
    c. automobile manufacturer's financing subsidiary.
    d. consumer finance companies.

21. The factor that usually sways a decision is favor of buying over leasing is
    a. monthly payment.
    b. termination fee.
    c. financing cost.
    d. down payment.

Name _____   Instructor _____

Date _____   Section _____

Experiential Problems

1. Using Exhibit 7.2 as a guide, prepare a needs and wants analysis for your college education. Even though you may be nearing the end of your college days this historical exercise may prove a useful guide for future decisions (graduate school for example). Be sure to consider the options that are/were available to you such as a two year community college vs. a four year state university vs. a four year private school.

   For example, your need is a degree in business which you could get with 2 years at a community college and 2 years at a state university. You have a want, however, to be a member of a fraternity for four years and this is not an option at your community college.

Need	Cost	Want	Cost
Bachelor's degree			
2 year-Community College	$4,000	Fraternity membership	$9,000*
2 year-State University	$12,000		

* This is the added cost of the first two years at a state university over a community college, fraternity initiation fee, dues, house fee and travel costs home.

2. Assuming that you will keep your current car for three years, prepare an analysis of your estimated cost to operate it for that period of time. To do this you will need to answer the following questions:

   a. Based on past experience and your plans for the next three years, how many miles will you drive?

   b. Factoring in you car's miles per gallon, your answer to part a, and the current cost of gasoline, compute your gasoline costs for the next three years.

   c. Find out the estimated insurance costs by calling your agent. Do they anticipate an increase in premiums? If your plans include moving to a different city or state what will this do to your insurance costs?

   d. Add in three year's license and inspection fees. Again consider the impact of any possible moves.

e. What repairs/replacements will your car require in three years? Factor in not only major but routine oil changes and lubes.

f. If your car is not paid for, contact your bank or whatever financial institution you financed with and find out the interest you will pay over the three years.

g. Do not overlook any other costs such as parking fees, university or county permits.

h. Add up the costs in part b through g and divide by the miles in calculated in part a, to get an operating cost per mile.

3. The text suggests some good do's and don'ts of car buying. To give you a feel for how good a job most people do or do not do buying a car, ask eight people the following questions. The questions are designed to elicit a yes or no response. If they do not understand part of the question be sure to explain it until they can give you a yes or no response.

    What percentage of the people did everything right? everything wrong? What did those not following the text's suggestion give as a reason? Does it appear a valid one?

Person	a	b	c	d	e	f	g	h
Did you shop at more than one dealer before buying?								
Did you negotiate up from the invoice price?								
Did you negotiate down from the sticker price?								
Did you buy any "Paks"?								
Did you shop around for financing?								

After you complete your analysis compare your needs and wants to the value you prioritized in chapter 1. Do they coincide? If not why?

Chapter 7 Solutions

What Do You Know?

1. F	6. T
2. F	7. T
3. T	8. F
4. T	9. F
5. T	10. F

Key Terminology Exercise - Crossword Puzzle

<u>Across</u>

2. small claims
5. want
6. need
7. invoice

<u>Down</u>

1. warranty
3. comparison
4. sticker

Multiple Choice Questions

1. c	11. d
2. b	12. b
3. d	13. a
4. e	14. a
5. c	15. d
6. d	16. d
7. c	17. c
8. d	18. d
9. c	19. b
10. b	20. b
	21. d

Chapter 8

The Housing Decision

What Do You Know?

T F 1. The down payment is not all the cash you will need to buy a house.

T F 2. Some people have two mortgages on one house.

T F 3. Good schools typically mean higher real estate or property taxes.

T F 4. Less than 2/3 of all American households live in owner-occupied, single family homes.

T F 5. Resale of condominiums is difficult.

T F 6. The best mortgages are 30 year, rather than 15 year.

T F 7. Adjustable rate mortgages are best for people who plan to stay in one house a long time.

T F 8. If you take out a home equity loan, you can only use it for expenses related to the house.

T F 9. You can't lose your house if you have kept up on the first mortgage, but defaulted on the home equity loan.

T F 10. Home ownership is always an excellent investment.

Chapter 8

The Housing Decision

Chapter Overview

Homes are no longer the guaranteed financial investment they once were. However, that should not discourage you from owning a home, but merely demonstrates how critical it has become to select the right home, in the right location, at the right price, with the right financing. A planned and informative decision includes not only determining how much you want to afford (remember housing needs vs. housing wants) but how much you are willing to pay for that privilege; i.e. calculate the total interest over the life of the loan.

Chapter Outline

I. Your Personal Housing Requirements

    A. Where do you want to live

        1. lifestyle

        2. commuting distance and time

        3. taxes

        4. public services

        5. schools

    B. Your financial resources

        1. housing should be no more than 1/3 take-home pay

        2. down payment - at least 10% purchase price

        3. closing costs - 2 1/2% of purchase price

    C. The kind of home you want and need

        1. bigger is not always better, but is usually more expensive

        2. don't pay for amenities you don't need

        3. housing needs change dramatically throughout the life cycle

II. Major Housing Options

    A. Single family homes

        1. average new home, 2,000 square feet, $135,000

2. average existing home $115,000

3. prices vary greatly throughout the country

B. Condominiums and co-ops

   1. 5% American families live in condos

   2. refers to a form of ownership, not a type of building

C. Manufactured homes

   1. used to be called mobile homes, but rarely are the homes moved

   2. occupied by less than 5% of American families

   3. average price $32,500

D. Rental option

   1. most are unfurnished

   2. found in any area in any form from individual rooms to complete houses

   3. average rent is under $600 a month

   4. least expensive in Midwestern small cities and rural areas

   5. lease defines rights and responsibilities of landlord and tenant

III. Buy vs Rent Decision

A. Rent advantages

   1. liquidity

   2. mobility

   3. some cost savings

B. Ownership advantages

   1. sense of belonging

   2. personal satisfaction

   3. final decision-making over changes

   4. potential investment

   5. tax savings

   6. forced way to save money

C. Buy vs rent worksheet

IV. Financing The Purchase of a Home

A. Home affordability worksheet

B. Down payment

   1. average for all buyers = 25%

      average for first time buyers = 10%

   2. PMI or private mortgage insurance guarantees the mortgage will be paid

C. Monthly payment

   1. mortgages are fully amortized with part of payment interest and part principal

   2. over the life of the loan, the % going to interest declines

D. Closing costs

   1. points

   2. prepaid interest

   3. sales commission

   4. title charges

E. Sources of mortgages

   1. FHA mortgages

   2. VA mortgages

   3. conventional mortgages

F. Types of mortgages

   1. 30 year fixed rate

   2. 15 year fixed rate

   3. adjustable rate

G. Refinancing a mortgage

   1. taking out a new loan to pay off old loan

   2. done to take advantage of lowered interest rates

   3. costs money to refinance

   4. good idea if new interest rate is 2% lower than old one

H. Second mortgages

   1. only consumer interest that is tax deductible

   2. more risky; higher interest rates; shorter terms

   3. can be used for a variety of reasons not related to the house

   4. home equity loans - like a revolving charge account or credit card, may borrow up to a credit limit without reapplying each time

V. Finding The Right House To Buy

    A. Preparing to buy

        1. pre-qualify for a mortgage

        2. use a realtor

        3. buyers typically look at 15 different homes

        4. make a formal offer

            a. price you are offering

            b. the date you want to purchase and the date you want to move in

            c. how long the offer is available

        5. receive an acceptance, counter offer, or rejection

        6. earnest money - security deposit

    B. Home inspections

    C. Home warranties

VI. Selling A Home

    A. Using a real estate agent vs ''sale by owner''

        1. realtors charge 6-7% selling price as a fee for their services

        2. realtor functions

            a. set a selling price

            b. advertise the house

            c. bring in potential buyers

            d. verify potential buyers can afford the house

            e. assist with negotiations

            f. work with the bank to ''close'' the deal and arrange financing

    B. Setting a selling price

    C. Selling costs

    D. Fixing up your home

    E. Taxes and the sale of your home

Name _____   Instructor _____

Date _____   Section _____

Key Terminology Exercise - Matching

Match the words in column A to the statements in column B.

<u>Column A</u>

A. Closing costs
B. Mortgage
C. Foreclosure
D. Condominium
E. Co-op apartment
F. Lease
G. Private mortgage insurance
H. Points
I. Earnest money
J. Equity

<u>Column B</u>

___ 1. Having a wild party at 3 am in your apartment may violate this document.

___ 2. This refers to the kind of ownership rather than the type of structure which may be a high rise, duplex or a variety of other forms.

___ 3. This may reduce your down payment to as low as 5%, but is expensive.

___ 4. For tax purposes these are considered interest but are technically a loan origination fee or a loan discount.

___ 5. These can amount to 2.5% of the cost of the house and increase the cash you will need to purchase a home.

___ 6. When asked if they own a home, many people answer ''Yes, me and the bank.'' This is the part they own.

___ 7. To show that your offer on a home is serious you will be asked to pay this.

___ 8. Failure to keep up your house payments may cause the bank to do this.

___ 9. What every homeowner will have unless they can pay cash for a home.

___ 10. A corporation where stock ownership equals home ownership.

Name _____   Instructor _____

Date _____   Section _____

Multiple Choice Questions

1. The biggest barrier to home ownership is
   a. the monthly payments.
   b. coming up with the necessary down payment.
   c. affording the upkeep on the house.
   d. closing costs.

2. One reason **not** to buy a home today is
   a. as an investment.
   b. as a place to live.
   c. for peace of mind.
   d. for tax savings.

3. When you buy a home you are always assured of
   a. being able to sell the house for what you paid for it.
   b. being able to sell the house for enough to pay off your loan.
   c. being able to sell the house for a profit.
   d. none of the above

4. The factor that most influences a person's housing decision is
   a. cost.
   b. interest rates.
   c. structure (brick, frame).
   d. location.

5. Which of the following should **not** be considered when deciding where to buy a home?
   a. how far it is to work
   b. the kind and quality of public services
   c. taxes
   d. schools
   e. none, they should all be considered

6. Your housing should consume no more of your take-home pay than
   a. 1/2   c. 1/4
   b. 1/3   d. 1/5

7. Home ownership has become more affordable in recent years because
   a. mortgage rates went down.
   b. housing costs declined.
   c. down payment requirements decreased.
   d. all of the above

8. If you wish to be a home owner you may choose from
    a. single-family detached home.
    b. high rise tower.
    c. garden apartment.
    d. all of the above

9. The median price of a single family home is around
    a. $100,000.
    b. $125,000.
    c. $150,000.
    d. $175,000.

10. Mortgages require the buyer to
    a. make regular payments.
    b. pay real estate taxes.
    c. pay insurance on the property.
    d. all of the above

11. Condominiums give you
    a. tax advantages from home ownerships.
    b. ready resale market due to large percentage of people living in condos.
    c. choice of housing type (high rise tower, duplex, row house, etc.).
    d. a and c, only

12. The Uniform Residential Landlord and Tenant Act spells out the obligations and rights of all **except**
    a. the landlord.
    b. the tenant.
    c. local government.
    d. all of the above

13. All of the following are advantages of renting **except**
    a. liquidity.
    b. mobility.
    c. tax advantages.
    d. certain cost savings.

14. Lenders do not wish to see your total principal, interest, taxes and insurance exceed
    a. 18% of gross monthly income.
    b. 28% of gross monthly income.
    c. 38% of gross monthly income.
    d. 48% of gross monthly income.

15. Who pays closing costs?
    a. negotiated between buyer and seller
    b. determined by law in the Uniform Settlement Statement
    c. usually a matter of local custom
    d. a and c, only

16. A 0% down payment is sometimes available with
    a. FHA mortgages.
    b. V.A. mortgages.
    c. conventional mortgages.
    d. none of the above

17. For a small fee which of the following will search for the best mortgage for your particular situation
    a. mortgage broker.
    b. realtor.
    c. banker.
    d. local VA administrator.

18. Adjustable Rate Mortgages are a good choice if
    a. you do not plan on staying long.
    b. interest rates decline over the life of the loan.
    c. you have a small down payment.
    d. a and b, only

19. Refinancing is considered advisable if the cost of refinancing divided by the reduction in your monthly payment
    a. exceeds 18.
    b. exceeds 12.
    c. is less than 18.
    d. is less than 28.

20. Second mortgages may be used to
    a. finance home improvements.
    b. finance a boat.
    c. finance a car.
    d. all of the above

21. To get the most back on your investments in home improvements, you should put your money into
    a. a swimming pool.
    b. remodeling the kitchen.
    c. remodeling the bathrooms.
    d. b and c, only

Name _____   Instructor _____

Date _____   Section _____

Experiential Problems

1. List all of the possible criteria a person might consider when selecting an area in which to live. Below is a partial list to get you started. List criteria even if they are currently not significant to you at this time.

    a. Partial list of criteria:

    close to schools   clean air
    quiet street   on or near water
    parks   others:
    shopping malls
    landscaping
    sidewalks
    street lights

b. After you have completed your list, review it carefully. List below, in order of importance to you, the top five criteria.

c. Refer to the values and goals you identified in chapter 1. Do your five criteria for a housing area coincide with your values and goals? Write a paragraph to explain why they do or do not coincide with your values and goals. Write a paragraph to explain why they do or do not coincide.

d. We live in a very mobile society and as a result most people move several times during their lives. Resale of homes is therefore, a consideration in selecting a housing area. Contact a realtor and discuss the impact on resale/value that each of the five criteria you select in b will have.

<u>Criteria</u>   <u>Impact on resale/value</u>

1.

2.

3.

4.

5.

2. In experiential problem #1, you addressed the question of what is important to you in a housing area. In this problem describe what your perfect house would look like. Type of construction, 2 story or ranch, basement are just a few of the issues you should cover in your description.

   a. Description of the perfect home.

   b. Using your description above and your location criteria in experiential problem #1, get a price range for your perfect house. You can get this by looking through the real estate ads in the local paper or by visiting with a realtor and giving them you requirements as to area and house.

      Price range $_____ to $_____

c. Assuming a 20% down payment and using the Home Affordability worksheet in Exhibit 8.3 in the text as a guide, work backwards up the worksheet to determine your gross monthly income needed to afford your perfect house.

Purchase price

Less 20% down payment —

Mortgage

Factor from mortgage table at 7.5% ÷

Mortgage payment

Lender's affordability ratio ÷

Gross monthly income

x 12 months

Annual income required to afford your perfect home*

*This figure would need to be higher as we have not factored in taxes and insurance.

d. Is the annual income you computed above (part c) consistant with the career choice you made in chapter 2 and the value and goals from chapter 1?

e. If your answer in d was no, prepare a wants and needs analysis of your perfect home. Based on your values and goals, what is a want and not a need?

3. Some banks offer mortgages with other than monthly payments. These may be bi-monthly (two payments each month) or bi-weekly (a payment every two weeks) and are usually 15 years. Obtain an amortization schedule for a 15 year $100,000 mortgage at 6.7% for the monthly and bi-monthly and 6.5% for the bi-weekly. You can obtain an amortization schedule at your local bank in most cases, or create your own in your school's computer lab.

   a. Is there any difference in the interest paid over the full term of the loan?

      15 year monthly compared to 15 year bi-monthly

   $_____difference

      15 year monthly compared to 15 year bi-weekly

   $_____difference

      15 year bi-monthly compared to 15 year bi-weekly

   $_____difference

   b. Briefly explain why each of these differences occur.

   c. Based on your amortization schedules how long does it take to pay off a:

      1. 15 year bi-monthly_____

      2. 15 year bi-weekly _____

   d. Explain your answer to c.

Chapter 8 Solutions

What Do You Know?

1. T	6. F
2. T	7. F
3. T	8. F
4. T	9. F
5. T	10. F

Key Terminology Exercise - Matching

1. F	6. J
2. D	7. I
3. G	8. C
4. H	9. B
5. A	10. E

Multiple Choice Questions

1. b	11. d
2. a	12. c
3. d	13. c
4. d	14. b
5. e	15. d
6. b	16. b
7. a	17. a
8. d	18. d
9. b	19. c
10. d	20. d
	21. d

Part 4

Purchasing Protection

Part 4

Purchasing Protection

Chapter 16 The Insurance Decision
Chapter 17 Life Insurance
Chapter 18 Health and Disability Insurance
Chapter 19 Property and Liability Insurance

Chapter 9

The Insurance Decision

What Do You Know?

T F 1. I know how much life, disability, auto, and liability coverage I currently have.

T F 2. Wearing seat belts is a way to deal with risk.

T F 3. It makes sense to buy life insurance when children are small because it is cheap.

T F 4. The best way to deal with risk is to transfer it to an insurance company.

T F 5. Not smoking cigarettes is a method for dealing with risk called avoidance.

T F 6. While there are things you can do to minimize some risks, you cannot totally eliminate them.

T F 7. Insurance is too depressing to think about.

T F 8. It's best to leave the amount of the insurance policy up to the insurance salesperson.

T F 9. Many people purchase the wrong types and amounts of insurance.

T F 10. Some risks are not even worth worrying about.

Chapter 9

The Insurance Decision

Chapter Overview

Insurance is a difficult topic to understand. Simply, there are two types of risk; only one type is insurable. You should identity all the possible risk situations you may encounter. Then, determine how you will deal with each of those risks. As insurance is only one of four ways to deal with risk, buying insurance is not the best option for all risks. This chapter defines basic risk and insurance concepts to lay the groundwork for studying the various kinds of insurance in the following three chapters.

Chapter Outline

I. The Concept of Risk

    A. Risk - uncertainty of injury/loss

        1. pure - possible loss but no possible gain

        2. speculative - possible loss or possible gain

    B. Ways of dealing with risk

        1. avoid it

        2. minimize it

        3. assume it

        4. transfer it

II. The Characteristics of an Insurable Risk

    A. Must be common to a large number of people
       (law of large numbers)

    B. Policyholder stands to suffer a financial loss
       (insurable interest)

    C. Loss cannot be expected or deliberately caused to happen
       (fortuitous loss)

    D. Loss must be measurable

    E. Risk should be spread over a wide geographical area

III. Major Categories of Insurance

    A. Life - protection against economic losses due to <u>premature</u> death

    B. Health and disability

    C. Property and liability

        1. auto
        2. homeowners
        3. personal liability

IV. Basic Elements of Insurance

    A. Insurance Premium

        1. underwriting - determining who to insure and what to charge
        2. insurance premium - payments made for insurance protection
        3. premiums decrease if you reduce your risk

    B. Insurance Policy - legally binding contract

        1. declarations
            a. what is being insured
            b. for how long
            c. for how much
            d. policy limits
            e. premium to be paid
            f. promises by the insured to lower the risk
        2. insuring agreements - coverage broadly defined
        3. exclusions - what the company won't pay for
        4. conditions - ground rules for both sides
        5. endorsements or riders - additions to customize the policy

    C. Insurance agent

        1. part of the premium you pay goes to the agent as a sales commission
        2. exclusive agents - sell policies offered by one company
        3. independent agents - sell policies from a variety of companies
        4. direct sellers - companies that sell policies directly and bypass agents

    D. Insurance company

        1. mutual insurance company - nonprofit organization owned by policy holders
        2. stock insurance company - profit seeking company owned by stockholders

V. The Insurance Purchase Process

   A. A risk management plan

      1. identify sources of risk

      2. evaluate each risk

      3. brainstorm ways to deal with each risk

      4. implement each choice

   B. What insurance do you need?

      1. life

      2. health

      3. disability

      4. homeowners

      5. auto

      6. personal liability

      7. insurance coverage may be determined by:

         a. law (mandatory auto liability)

         b. contract (mortgage contract requires homeowner's insurance)

         c. if the potential loss could lead to bankruptcy

   C. Where to buy the policy

      1. get general information

      2. obtain several quotes

      3. select company and agent

   D. How to buy the policy

   E. Resolving disputes with insurance companies

Name _____   Instructor _____

Date _____   Section _____

Key Terminology Exercise - Crossword Puzzle

Using the words found in the Running Glossary, complete the crossword puzzle. An X indicates a space between words in a multi-word answer. Clues for the puzzle are on the next page.

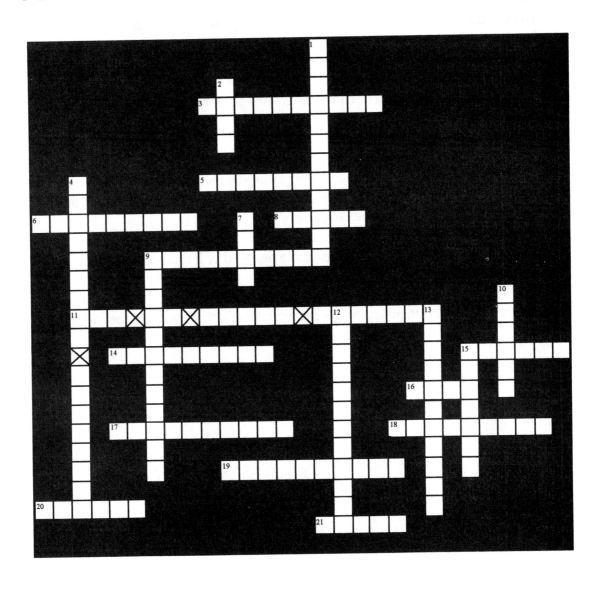

Across

3. If you break your leg and can't work, this insurance will help pay the bills.
5. This insurance covers your house, TV, VCR, furniture, etc.
6. the method most people use to deal with pure risk.
8. A for profit insurance company.
9. Losses that the insurance company specifically will not cover.
11. This makes an event predictable for a group but not for an individual.
14. If a risk is common to a large number of people it is this.
15. To answer questions about your insurance you would refer to this document.
16. This is a "no win" risk.
17. The ground rules agreed to by the insurance company and the insured.
18. If someone falls and is injured in your house you will need this kind of insurance.
19. An insurable loss.
20. A nonprofit insurance company.
21. This person may represent one company exclusively or may be independent and represent more than one.

Down

1. Basic descriptive information about an insurance policy.
2. This insurance will give you peace of mind, but the financial benefit will go to others.
4. You cannot take out a life insurance policy on a stranger because you lack this.
7. For this to exist, there must be uncertainty.
9. These are designed to meet the special needs of the insured.
10. Rising hospital costs and doctor fees make this kind of insurance essential.
12. The amount of premium to charge is determined by this process.
13. With this risk you can win or lose.
15. The costs of the insurance company are expressed in this charge to the insured.

Name _____   Instructor _____

Date _____   Section _____

Multiple Choice Questions

1. The amount paid out of every consumer dollar for insurance is
   a. 5 cents.   c. 25 cents.
   b. 12 cents.   d. 40 cents.

2. The number of Americans that make mistakes when buying insurance is
   a. 9 out of 10.
   b. 5 out of 10.
   c. 2 out of 10.
   d. too small to measure.

3. All risks have
   a. possibility of loss.
   b. uncertainty.
   c. possibility of gain.
   d. a and b, only

4. Investing your money into a new business venture exposes you to a(n)
   a. insurable risk.
   b. speculative risk.
   c. pure risk.
   d. all of the above

5. Investing your money in a home exposes you to a(n)
   a. insurable risk.
   b. speculative risk.
   c. pure risk.
   d. a and c, only

6. Not traveling by airplane is dealing with the risk of being killed or injured in a plane crash by
   a. avoiding risk.
   b. minimizing risk.
   c. assuming risk.
   d. transferring the risk.

7. Fastening your seat belt is dealing with the risk of being killed or injured in a car crash by
   a. avoiding risk.
   b. minimizing risk.
   c. assuming risk.
   d. transferring the risk.

8. If you ignore the risk of becoming ill and not being able to work, you are dealing with the risk of loss of income by
    a. avoiding risk.
    b. minimizing risk.
    c. assuming risk.
    d. transferring the risk.

9. Buying fire insurance is dealing with the risk of your house burning down by
    a. avoiding risk.
    b. minimizing risk.
    c. assuming risk.
    d. transferring the risk.

10. All of the following are necessary for a risk to be insurable **except**
    a. predictable on a group basis.
    b. insurable interest must exist.
    c. the loss must be expected and not accidental.
    d. the loss must be measurable.

11. Most homeowner insurance covers you for all of the following **except**
    a. fire.
    b. earthquake.
    c. windstorm.
    d. burglary.

12. Your apartment is burglarized when someone breaks through the front door. The damaged door will be paid for by
    a. you, out-of-pocket.
    b. your homeowners (renters) insurance.
    c. your landlord, out-of-pocket.
    d. your landlord's insurance.

13. Person A pays less in automobile insurance premiums than person B because
    a. A is 49 years old and B is 19.
    b. A is female and B is male.
    c. A lives in Podunk, Iowa and B lives in Chicago.
    d. all of the above

14. An insurance policy contains all of the following **except**
    a. declarations.
    b. insuring agreements.
    c. premium rate structure.
    d. exclusions.

15. You may purchase insurance from all of the following **except**
    a. an agent who works for one company.
    b. an agent who represents several companies.
    c. through an insurance companies 800 number.
    d. at Sears and Roebuck.

16. To avoid mistakes in making an insurance decision you must
    a. know what to insure.
    b. how much insurance to buy.
    c. how long to insure it.
    d. all of the above

Name _____ Instructor _____

Date _____ Section _____

Experiential Problems

1. Selecting an insurance agent can be a very important decision in your financial planning. An informational interview is a good way to gather data to make this decision. Contact an insurance agent and ask for an appointment to do your interview. Prepare your questions in advance and make notes as the agent answers your questions.

    Here are some suggested questions. This list is by no means exhaustive, so add those you would find helpful in making a decision.

    1. How long have you been an insurance agent?

    2. What formal training have you had?

    3. What certifications do you have?

    4. What did you have to do to get certified?

    5. Do you represent only one company or several?

    6. What kinds of insurance do you sell (life, auto, etc.)?

    7. What services do you offer that I can not get if I deal with a direct sell (800 number)?

    8. How often do you meet with your clients?

    9. How are your companies rated by Best?

    10. What else can you tell me that might help me to decide where to buy my insurance?

2. Using Exhibit 9.6 in your text as a guide, do a risk management plan for yourself.

    Step 1.   Identify sources of risk - do a detailed walk-around of your house, apartment or dorm room. In a notebook, answer the three questions in step 1 of the exhibit. Carry the notebook with you to work and class for a day or two to complete this step. Consolidate your data in the notebook and enter it on the worksheet.

    Step 2.   Evaluate the risk - how likely is the peril to occur or probability of loss can be determined by referring to statistical data or just applying common sense and logic in some cases. Putting a dollar figure on the loss and the impact of that amount on your finances will deal with the severity of the loss.

    Step 3.   Determine how to deal with risk - this is a highly personal decision and will be impacted by your value and goals in chapter 1 and your attitude toward risk.

    Step 4.   Implement your plan - put into action your decisions in step 3.

Step 1			Step 2		Step 3			
Identify what's at risk	Why it's at risk	Perils it faces	Probability of loss	Severity of loss	Avoid Risk	Control losses	Reduce risk	Transfer risk
(example) stereo in dorm room	Door easy to break open. -Room mate forgets to lock door.	Theft.	Few thefts in our dorm. Low.	It's old but $200 is replacement. $200 = moderate			Get room mate to lock room.	

Chapter 9 Solutions

What Do You Know?

1. T
2. T
3. F
4. F
5. T
6. T
7. F
8. F
9. T
10. T

Key Terminology Exercise - Crossword Puzzle

Across
3. disability
5. property
6. insurance
8. stock
9. exclusions
11. law of large numbers
14. insurable
15. policy
16. pure
17. conditions
18. liability
19. fortuitous
20. mutual
21. agent

Down
1. declarations
2. life
4. insurable interest
7. risk
9. endorsements
10. health
12. underwriting
13. speculative
15. premium

Multiple Choice Questions

1. b
2. a
3. d
4. b
5. d
6. a
7. b
8. c
9. d
10. c
11. c
12. d
13. d
14. c
15. d
16. d

Chapter 10

Life Insurance

What Do You Know?

T F 1. There is no way, other than life insurance, to be protected in case of death.

T F 2. I believe everyone should have life insurance.

T F 3. I believe in buying the credit life policy that is offered when you finance a car or a house.

T F 4. I am one of the few people who doesn't understand life insurance.

T F 5. Age is the most important factor in determining how much life insurance you need.

T F 6. Some people buy life insurance because it's an indicator of being "a good provider."

T F 7. I believe the more you pay for life insurance, the better the policy or protection.

T F 8. If a person dies as a result of an accident, many policies will double or triple the coverage.

T F 9. Insurance policies vary widely in cost for the same coverage.

T F 10. The older you are, the more life insurance you need.

Chapter 10

Life Insurance

Chapter Overview

Life insurance is viewed by many as American as motherhood and apple pie, but in fact we, as consumers, know very little about it. We made many assumptions about life insurance which cost us a lot of money, yet leave us with peace of mind and inappropriate protection. This chapter will challenge some of what you always believed about life insurance. This current and valid information should allow you to make decisions that, although may differ from what your family and friends believe, will put you in a better financial and more protected position.

Chapter Outline

I.   Why Purchase Life Insurance?

   A. Cash for immediate needs after a death

   B. Readjustment funds

   C. Replacement income

   D. Special situations

II. How Much Life Insurance Do You Need?

III. Types of Life Insurance Policies

   A. Term

      1. provides only protection; no savings

      2. least expensive

      3. offers financial protection for a specified number of years in event of death

   B. Whole life

      1. provides protection and savings (cash value)

      2. insurance company invests the excess money you pay for this type

      3. purchased for you entire life

      4. may borrow against whole life policies which reduces protection level

C. Universal life insurance

    1. provides term protection and tax-deferred savings that earns interest at competitive rates

    2. may borrow money but does not reduce protection level as the money comes out of the savings/investment portion

D. Other life insurance options

    1. group life insurance

    2. variable life insurance

    3. credit life insurance

        a. decreasing term insurance

        b. <u>very</u> expensive

E. Which type of life insurance is right for you?

    1. recommend anyone under 50 purchase term

    2. never use life insurance as an investment

IV. The Life Insurance Contract

A. The beneficiary clause

B. Settlement options

    1. life income

    2. fixed income

    3. interest only

C. Premium payment clause

D. Dividend clause

    1. receive cash

    2. reduce premiums

    3. buy additional insurance

E. Accidental death clause

F. Suicide clause

G. Waiver-of-premium clause

H. Guaranteed insurability clause

I. Non-forfeiture option

J. Policy reinstatement

V. Buying Life Insurance

    A. Making cost comparisons

        1. premium per $1,000 coverage

        2. net cost method

        3. interest-adjusted cost index method

    B. Choosing the right company and agent

Name _____   Instructor _____

Date _____   Section _____

Key Terminology Exercise - Word Search

Read the list of words below, then locate them in the puzzle. The words are in all directions: vertically, horizontally, diagonally, backward. Circle each word found, then strike it off the list.

```
W W U D K T I O F C N D U R W T O I A K U D H B R O R I
L B H S M L E Z Y R A I C I F E N E B W A S I E M Z A L
N R C O I N E R Y S A S R I G Y V O K D I G O U U S I F
K G I U L K O R M L K V H S O O L O S C S O K N I L S O
D S O Z K E Z R O I E Z H V Z K R Z I T S Z W I M R H E
S W K S E E L D N I N S W K A M D S Z U M S D R E D I Y
A K W E R A L I I X A S K I T L X L S N N E C E R X O T
Z L D R S Z R I F C X E U O R B U R L D O E T W P C K I
X R C D K X D T F E C D S R D L E E O A K D A H F F W N
C E F X O C X T O E I X E K A O T H D A W X T C O T D M
V C R C L V C Y E Y A N C D X N T C X N D C G O R D C E
B M T F R B F T R T E O S C F E C F S H C F A L E O F D
E L G T E E T G E G U T M U M E T E K Y F T A A V G R N
U R A Y Q U Y V Q V N Y R T R Q V H O U R Y N S I V T I
G U A R A N T E E D I N S U R A B I L I T Y C L A U S E
I E N G N I G H N H R O E G G C N I T M G R Y A W H A L
R T H V B R V O B O C V T A V B S C G I A A U N S O A B
E H Y B L E B L L T W B H A B L L U E I A I J N A L N U
W K U H R W H S E S N H K N H R S B T A N D M I E S H O
A L J U L N O N F O R F E I T U R E O P T I O N R T Y D
Q S M L E Q L B E B R L S Y L E B O O W Y F I V O B U G
U N I V E R S A L L I F E I N S U R A N C E A E F T J H
L W I T F L T O F N A T W J T F M T S E J B L R E I M R
K V A R I A B L E L I F E I N S U R A N C E R S R O W E
```

WORD LIST

BENEFICIARY
CASH VALUE
DOUBLE INDEMNITY
GUARANTEED INSURABILITY CLAUSE
NET COST METHOD
NONFORFEITURE OPTION

TERM INSURANCE
UNIVERSAL LIFE INSURANCE
VARIABLE LIFE INSURANCE
WAIVER OF PREMIUM
WHOLE LIFE INSURANCE

Name _____   Instructor _____

Date _____   Section _____

Multiple Choice Questions

1. The only life insurance that has no cash value is
    a. whole.
    b. term.
    c. universal.
    d. variable.

2. The amount of life insurance a person needs depends on
    a. a person's age.
    b. family situation.
    c. accumulated assets.
    d. all of the above

3. The appropriate amount of life insurance is
    a. highly individual.
    b. an easy and exact computation.
    c. a multiple of earnings.
    d. a and c, only

4. In computing your life insurance needs you should factor in
    a. social security benefits your children will receive.
    b. company pension death benefits.
    c. income of spouse.
    d. all of the above

5. As you get older your life insurance needs will
    a. increase.
    b. increase then decrease.
    c. decrease.
    d. decrease then increase.

6. If you want a savings feature along with protection you must buy
    a. whole life.
    b. term life.
    c. universal life.
    d. a and c, only

7. Typically for persons under 55 the least expensive form of life insurance is
    a. whole life.
    b. term life.
    c. universal life.
    d. a and c, only

8. Level term insurance provides all of the following **except**
    a. premiums that remain constant.
    b. fixed amount of insurance.
    c. coverage for a specific period of time.
    d. a good return on your cash value.

9. If your insurance need is the college education of your three children the most appropriate choice is
    a. decreasing term.
    b. level term.
    c. whole life.
    d. universal life.

10. Deposit term life insurance is one of the cheapest forms of term insurance if
    a. you keep the policy for only a short period of time.
    b. you keep the policy for its full term.
    c. you renew the policy at least once.
    d. you don't buy one as they are very expensive.

11. All of the following are whole-life insurance **except**
    a. straight life.
    b. limited-payment.
    c. universal.
    d. all are whole-life.

12. Funds borrowed on life insurance policies can be used for any of the following **except**
    a. a trip to Las Vegas.
    b. medical expenses.
    c. education expenses.
    d. all of the above

13. Universal life features
    a. term insurance protection.
    b. tax deferred savings.
    c. competitive return on savings.
    d. all of the above

14. The percentage of group life insurance policies in force today is
    a. under 20%.
    b. about 40%.
    c. over 50%.
    d. nearly 70%.

15. Credit life insurance is all of the following **except**
    a. a guarantee that your debt will be repaid.
    b. decreasing term life.
    c. cheaper than conventional term.
    d. available for the length of time the loan is outstanding.

16. The return earned on the savings feature of whole life policies is
    a. for less than that available on money market funds.
    b. about the same as corporate bonds.
    c. more than on common stock.
    d. one of the best available on any investment.

17. Life insurance contracts contain all of the following **except**
    a. beneficiary clause.
    b. settlement options.
    c. premium payment clause.
    d. guaranteed dividend payment clause.

18. Suicide is
    a. specifically excluded from coverage.
    b. not covered if it occurs in the first two years.
    c. covered no matter when it occurs.
    d. is only covered if insanity is proven.

19. If your policy lapses, you can reinstate is by
    a. paying the premiums plus interest.
    b. providing proof of insurability.
    c. typically take action within one year.
    d. all of the above

Name _____   Instructor _____

Date _____   Section _____

Experiential Problems

1. Most people will at sometime in their life be offered credit life insurance which the authors indicate is a very expensive form of insurance protection.

    a. Describe the next situation where you will probably be offered credit life insurance.

    b. Call the kind of financial institution that will be dealt with and find out the cost of the credit life that you will probably be offered based on your answer to a.

    c. What alternatives to credit life insurance can you identify to deal with this risk? Determine or estimate a cost for each.

    Example: one alternative is a decreasing term life policy. Call an insurance agent, give them the amount and length of time involved and some personal information (age, sex, etc) and get a rough quote on premiums.

d. Based on your analysis of costs and alternatives, do you think you will accept or reject the credit life policy? Write a brief justification of your answer. Do not forget the personal values you established in chapter 1 and their impact on your answer.

2. Interview five people, one each from the following age groups: 25 to 35, 36 to 45, 46 to 55, 56 to 65 and over 65. Ask them the following questions:

	25 to 35	36-45	46-55	56-65	over 65
1. Do you have life insurance? If not why? If the answer to #1 is "no" ask question 2; if "yes" ask questions 3 through 6.					
2. What financial alternatives to life insurance do you have in your financial plan? Explain.					
3. How much life insurance coverage do you have?					
4. What kind(s) of policy(s) do you have—term, whole life, universal?					
5. What was the reason for the purchase of the policy(s)? Primary Secondary					
6. How do you see your life insurance portfolio changing in the future?					

3. Using some insurance coverage that you currently have (car insurance, household, life) do a cost comparison to determine if you are getting the most "bang" for your insurance buck.

   With your policy in hand call or visit two or three other insurance companies or independent agents and request a price quote for the coverage you currently have. Ask them to not alter or add coverage as this will make a price comparison difficult. Be sure to ask for explanations as to why price differences occur.

   To determine where to go for these price comparisons talk to friends, relatives, or simply go through the yellow pages.

Features (coverage)	Current Policy	Company A	Company B	Company C

Chapter 10 Solutions

What Do You Know?

1.	F	6.	T
2.	F	7.	F
3.	F	8.	T
4.	F	9.	T
5.	F	10.	F

Key Terminology Exercise - Word Search

```
W W U D K T I O F C N D U R W T O I A K U D H B R O R I
L B H S M L E Z Y R A I C I F E N E B W A S I E M Z A L
N R C O I N E R Y S A R R I G Y V O K D I G O U U S I F
K G I U L K O R M L K V H S O O L O S C S O K N I L S O
D S O Z K E Z R O I E Z H Z Z K R Z I T S Z W I M R H E
S W K S E E D N I N S W K A M D S Z U M S D R E D I Y
A K W E R A L I I X A S K I T L X L S N N E C E R X O T
Z L D R S Z R I F C X E U O R B U R L O O E T W P C K I
X R C D K X D T F E C D S R D L E E O A K D A H F F W N
C E F X O C X T O E I X E K A O T H D A W X T C O T D M
V C R C L V C Y E Y A N C D X T C X N D C G O R D C E
B M T F R B F T R T E O S C F E C F S H C F A L E O F D
E L G T E E T G E G U T M U M E T E K Y F T A A V G R N
U R A Y Q U Y V Q V N Y R T R Q V H O U R Y N S I V T I
G U A R A N T E E D I N S U R A B I L I T Y C L A U S E
I E N G N I G H N H R O E G G C N I T M G R Y A W H A L
R T H V B R V O B O V T A V B S C G I A A U N S O A B
E H Y B L E B L L T W B H A B L L U E I A I J N A L N U
W K U H R W H S E S N H K N H R S B T A N D M I E S H O
A L J U L N O N F O R F E I T U R E O P T I O N R T Y D
Q S M L E Q L B E B R L S Y L E B O O W Y F I V O B U G
U N I V E R S A L L I F E I N S U R A N C E A E F T J H
L W I T F L T O F N A T W J T F M T S E J B L R E I M R
K V A R I A B L E L I F E I N S U R A N C E R S R O W E
```

Multiple Choice Questions

1.	b	11.	c
2.	d	12.	d
3.	d	13.	d
4.	d	14.	b
5.	b	15.	c
6.	d	16.	a
7.	b	17.	d
8.	d	18.	b
9.	a	19.	d
10.	b		

Chapter 11

Health and Disability Insurance

What Do You Know?

T F 1. I know the deductibles and co-pays of my health care insurance.

T F 2. I understand the coordination of benefits between my auto insurance and health insurance.

T F 3. The head(s) of my household is(are) covered by disability income insurance.

T F 4. Dental insurance stresses preventive care, while not all health insurance does.

T F 5. Health insurance offered at work is generally less expensive than buying health insurance as a private individual.

T F 6. HMOs provide the best possible medical care.

T F 7. PPOs afford you limited choices in health care.

T F 8. If a medical procedure is covered by your health policy, your insurance company will pay whatever the doctor charges.

T F 9. Dental plans are rarely worth the cost unless your employer picks up a large share of the premium.

T F 10. You must be over 65 to qualify for Medicare.

Chapter 11

Health and Disability Insurance

Chapter Overview

Health care insurance is a hotly debated topic these days, partly because health care costs are expensive and have risen dramatically. As costs continue to escalate, health care has become the most valued fringe benefit among employees, as purchasing health care individually can be complicated and expensive.

Employers have reacted to rising costs in a number of ways: reducing coverage, decreasing payments, or adding less costly options such as managed care. This chapter will manuever you through the health care maze and assist you in choosing the right plan. Attention is also given to the neglected area of disability coverage.

Chapter Outline

I. The Need for Health Care Coverage

    A. The cost of U.S. health care

    B. Causes of rising health care costs

        1. demographics

        2. advances in medical technology

        3. litigation

        4. rising administrative costs

    C. Who pays our health care bills?

II. Providers of Health Care Coverage

    A. Private group health insurance

        1. includes basic coverage, major medical, and disability

        2. lower costs/more comprehensive coverage

        3. employer-sponsored full or partial

        4. deductible required

        5. COBRA

B. Individual health coverage

    1. more expensive

    2. must show evidence of insurability

C. Government programs

    1. Medicare - federal health insurance program for elderly and disabled

    2. Medicaid - medical assistance for low-income people by federal and state governments; benefits vary from state to state

III. Managed Care Programs

A. Health maintenance organizations (HMO)

    1. provides health care, not insurance

    2. owns the facility and doctors are employees

    3. emphasizes preventive care

B. Preferred provider organizations (PPO)

    1. negotiated contract between local physicians and hospitals and an employer to provide medical care at agreed upon rates

C. Assessing managed care programs

IV. Understanding Your Health Care Plan

A. Terms and provisions

    1. who's covered

    2. time period

    3. coordination of benefits

    4. second opinions and prior approvals

    5. policy limits

    6. deductibles and co-payments

    7. filing claims

B. Coverage provided

    1. most health plans are comprehensive, meaning the same plan covers hospital, surgical, physician and drug bills

    2. items not covered typically involve cosmetic surgery, experimental treatments, organ transplants, and pre-existing conditions

    C. Choosing the right plan for you

        1. cost

        2. choice and access

        3. differences in coverage

        4. patient satisfaction

    D. Vision and dental insurance

V. Disability Income Insurance

    A. Sources

        1. Social Security

        2. private group plan

        3. private individual plan

        4. the most overlooked from of insurance

    B. Determining how much disability insurance you need

        1. estimate monthly expenses if you became disabled

        2. add up currently available sources of monthly income if you became disabled

        3. subtract the above numbers and the difference is the amount of monthly disability coverage you need from a disability income policy

    C. Terms and provisions

        1. initial and secondary claims

        2. waiting period

        3. length of payment

        4. Social Security rider

        5. cost-of-living arrangements

    D. Workers' compensation

        1. disability benefits

        2. medical costs

        3. death benefits

Name _____   Instructor _____

Date _____   Section _____

Key Terminology Exercise - Matching

Match the words in column A to the statements in column B.

Column A

A. Fee for service (Indemnity plan)

B. Health maintenance organization (HMO)

C. Preferred provider organization (PPO)

D. Deductible

E. Co-payment

F. Reasonable and customary

G. Pre-exsisting condition

Column B

__ 1. A clause in your health insurance requiring you to pay $400 in medical costs before the insurance company will make any payments.

__ 2. The asthma that you have had since early childhood is excluded from coverage when you apply for health insurance because it is classified as this.

__ 3. With this kind of health care arrangement you have some choices in physcian and facilities while still receiving maximum available coverage.

__ 4. An alternative to health insurance, these provide all of your health care needs for a fixed fee but eliminate your choice in physicans and health care facilities.

__ 5. If your health insurance pays 90% of covered charges, this is the remaining 10% that you will pay.

__ 6. Traditional Blue Cross/Blue Shield programs are an example of this kind of health insurance.

__ 7. Insurance companies may not pay the total cost of an operation if it exceeds this amount.

Name _____   Instructor _____

Date _____   Section _____

Multiple Choice Questions

1. The most overlooked for insurance is
    a. major medical.
    b. disability income.
    c. dental.
    d. vision.

2. Health care insurance decisions are important because
    a. health care is expensive and gets more so annually.
    b. it is a complicated decision.
    c. it impacts your financial well being.
    d. all of the above

3. Since 1970, the average amount that each man, woman, and child on average spends on health care has gone up about
    a. 2 times.
    b. 5 times.
    c. 10 times.
    d. 15 times.

4. The rise in health care costs compared to the rise in overall inflation has been about
    a. half.
    b. the same.
    c. more than twice.
    d. over five times.

5. Over the next 5 to 10 years, economists expect all of the following to occur **except**
    a. the rate of increase in medical costs will slow down.
    b. medical care costs will increase greater than the overall inflation rate.
    c. personal income will grow at a faster rate than medical costs.
    d. none of the above

6. All of the following are given as reasons for rising health care costs **except**
    a. there are more younger people in the population today and they use more health care services.
    b. better drugs and more complex procedures only come at a higher price.
    c. people pay less of their own health care costs and have less incentive to keep costs down.
    d. more frequent lawsuits increase malpractice insurance premiums for doctors and hospitals.

7. The largest percentage of health care costs today are paid by
   a. individuals.
   b. private health insurance companies.
   c. government.
   d. others.

8. Since 1970, the percentage of total health care costs paid out-of-pocket by individuals has
   a. decreased slightly.
   b. decreased sharply.
   c. increased sharply.
   d. increased slightly.

9. The majority of people in America today have
   a. no health insurance coverage.
   b. are covered by Medicare and Medicaid.
   c. have private individual health insurance.
   d. have private group health insurance.

10. Group health insurance became popular because
    a. it was part of Roosevelt's New Deal.
    b. it was a good way to atract workers during WWII when wages were controlled.
    c. it was part of Johnson's Great Society.
    d. employers demanded it in the 1950's.

11. What is the percentage of private companies and governemental units offering at least some form of group health insurance today?
    a. 20%
    b. 40%
    c. 60%
    d. 80%

12. The advantage of group health insurance over individual plans is
    a. it costs less.
    b. better coverage.
    c. for people with pre-existing conditions it may be their only option.
    d. all of the above

13. Under COBRA, employers are required by law to
    a. continue coverage for up to 18 months for laid off workers.
    b. continue coverage for up to 36 months for widows, divorced spouses and their dependents.
    c. pay a portion of th premiums.
    d. a and b, only

14. HMOs work to reduce health care costs by
    a. emphasizing preventive medical care.
    b. avoiding unnecessary operations and tests.
    c. stressing health education and shortened hospital stays.
    d. all of the above

15. Even with health insurance we may still be faced with a big medical bill because of
    a. deductibles.
    b. co-payments.
    c. reasonable and customary charge limits.
    d. the combination of a, b and c.

16. The premium on an individual disability income policy should be approximately this percentage of the income that it will replace
    a. 2%
    b. 5%
    c. 7%
    d. 10%

17. Workers' compensation varies from state to state and may be provided through
    a. private insurance.
    b. self-insurance.
    c. state insurance funds.
    d. all of the above

Name _____   Instructor _____

Date _____   Section _____

Experiential Problems

1. a. Develop a profile of a person who would prefer each of the three basic kinds of health care plans.

Fee for service	PPO	HMO

b. Find a company that offers a variety of health care plans (fee for service, PPO, HMO) to their employees. The larger the company the greater the variety of health care plans available to employees so try to use a major company for your information source. Get information on the plans and determine which you would select. Explain the reasons for your choice.

c. What developments or changes might occur in your own situation in five to ten years that may cause you to shift from the plan you selected in b to one of the other plans? To which plan might you shift? Explain your selection.

2. Using the budget that you developed in the End of Chapter Problems in Chapter 3, complete the worksheet below. If you are not employed prepare the worksheet for a freind or family member.

   a. List and evaluate the options open to you or the person for whom the worksheet was prepared to deal with the need for disability insurance.

Worksheet
Estimating Disability Insurance Needs

Line	Monthly Expenses if Disabled	Your Figures
1	Housing	
2	Utilities	
3	Food	
4	Other living expenses	
5	Medical & dental care	
6	Contribution to college fund	
7	Insurance & loan payments	
8	Total expenses (sum of lines 1 through 7)	

Current Sources of Monthly Income if Disabled

Line		Your Figures
9	Social Security	$1,000
10	Other government sources	
11	Group disability payments	
12	Worker's compensation	
13	Spouse's take home income	
14	Other income	
15	Total income (sum of lines 9 through 14)	
16	**Disability Insurance Needs (line 8 minus line 15)**	

3. Interview four friends or relatives - two who have a fee for service plan and two who have a managed care plan. Rephrase the pro and cons found in Exhibit 11.7 (reproduced below) as the basis for your questions.

Exhibit 11.7

Comparing a Fee-for-Service to a Managed Care Plan

	Fee for Service Plans	**Managed Care Plans**
Pros	• Almost unlimited choice of doctors, hospitals, and other providers of health care services. • Easy access to medical specialists. • Can change doctors whenever desired. • Fewer limits on tests and diagnostic procedures.	• Little if any paperwork. • Less out of pocket expenses. • No wait in getting reimbursed. • Possibly lower monthly premiums. • Often pay for routine physicals and immunizations.
Cons	• Higher out of pocket expenses (deductibles and co-payments). • Possibility higher monthly premiums. • More paperwork and delays in getting reimbursed. • Potentially more disputes with insurance company over charges. • Often will not pay for routine physicals and immunizations.	• Choice of doctors, hospitals and other providers of health care services much more limited. • More difficult to change doctors. Access to specialists restricted. • Limits on tests on diagnostic procedures. • Delays possible in obtaining emergency care.

Note: Fee-for-service and managed care plans vary widely. Items listed above are general and may not apply to every specific health care plan.

a. Enter your questions and responses below.

Fee-for-service

Question	Person 1	Person 2

Managed care plan

Question	Person 3	Person 4

b. Based on the responses to your questions, would you change your selection of plans in experiential problem #1? Explain your answer.

Chapter 11 Solutions

What Do You Know?

1. T
2. T
3. T
4. T
5. T

6. F
7. F
8. F
9. T
10. F

Key Terminology Exercise - Matching

1. D
2. G
3. C
4. B
5. E
6. A
7. F

Multiple Choice Questions

1. b
2. d
3. c
4. c
5. c
6. a
7. c
8. b
9. d
10. b

11. d
12. d
13. d
14. d
15. d
16. a
17. d

Experiential Problems

1. a. There is no completely right or wrong answer. The following are possible profiles for each category.

Fee-for-service	PPO	HMO
1. Health care needs are not excessive	1. Value some cost savings but not primary	1. Will not or cannot make health care decision
2. Take an active role in health and health care	2. Prefer options in serious situations	2. Not easily frustrated by bureacrity delays
3. People who like to research alternatives and have control over final decisions	3. Prefer routine decisions be made for them	3. Place great trust in primary care physician
4. Put premium on latest medical procedures	4. Has widely varying medical needs in family	4. Dislike paperwork
5. Customize own health care		5. Do not wish to worry about paying for service not covered
6. Value personal relationship with medical caregivers		
7. Only go to doctor when absolutely necessary		
8. Will seek out "best" available doctors and facilities, regardless of location		

Chapter 12

Property and Liability Insurance

What Do You Know?

T F 1. I'm a renter so I don't need liability insurance.

T F 2. Auto insurance rates do not vary from company to company within the same location.

T F 3. I need more liability insurance as I accumulate more assets.

T F 4. I am not responsible for damages my children may cause.

T F 5. I should always carry comprehensive and collision insurance on my car.

T F 6. I can only be held liable if I'm negligent.

T F 7. I can't be sued for more than the amount of my liability insurance.

T F 8. A no-fault insurance state means I can't be sued for damages.

T F 9. Raising my deductibles is a good way to lower my premiums.

T F 10. Maintaining a high GPA can lower my car insurance premiums.

Chapter 12

Property and Liability Insurance

Chapter Overview

Homeowners and automobile insurance are inseparable from the concept of liability, which is the financial responsibility one person has to another. The application of the definition of liability has expanded dramatically, particularly in the last 10 years. People are now being sued if they make someone else feel uncomfortable. Many years ago if you were injured by a piece of machinery, it was regarded as your fault for being "in the way" and in no way was anyone else to blame.

Today our culture is more prone to litigation. It is your responsibility to thoroughly examine your personal liability risks in your daily life and be certain you are adequately protected, typically through your homeowners and auto insurance policies.

Chapter Outline

I.   The Concept of Liability

    A. Negligence

        1. failure to exercise care

        2. failure to do what a reasonable person would do is called reasonable care

    B. Strict liability

        1. responsible but not directly at fault

        2. example: keeping an aggressive animal who bites your neighbor

    C. Vicarious liability

        1. negligent but not involved in the negligent act

        2. example: your child damages someone else's property

II. Personal Liability Insurance

    A. Homeowners comprehensive personal liability insurance

        1. part of homeowners policy

        2. covers family and pets

        3. personal injuries or property losses

B. Automobile liability insurance

    1. part of auto policy

    2. covers medical and repair bills

    3. required in most states

C. Umbrella policy

    1. excess personal liability protection

    2. $1 million or more total coverage

    3. false arrest, libel, invasion of privacy, and defamation of character

    4. supplements homeowners and auto policies

IV. Homeowners Insurance

A. What a homeowners policy covers

    1. damage to the house

    2. damage to other structures

    3. damage to trees and shrubs

    4. personal property losses

    5. additional living expenses

    6. liability

    7. no-fault medical payments and damages

B. Understanding a standard homeowners policy

    1. standard policies

        a. insurance industry has established 6 different policies

        b. policies differ in 2 ways
           -number of perils covered
           -are perils included or excluded

    2. how much coverage should you have

        a. 80% current replacement value

        b. full replacement coverage is recommended as it will repair/replace entire structure

    3. deductible

        a. higher the deductible, lower the premium

        b. $250 standard deductible

    4. Renter's and condominium policies

        a. household contents and personal property

        b. less than 1/3 of renters are insured

C. Supplementing the homeowners policy

    1. endorsements

    2. floaters

D. Miscellaneous insurance protection

    1. flood insurance

    2. earthquake insurance

E. Recording your personal property

F. What to do if you have a claim against your policy

IV. Automobile Insurance

A. Types of coverage

    1. bodily injury and property damage liability insurance

        a. covers insured if his/her car injures or kills and/or damages property

        b. covers anyone with permission to drive insured vehicle

        c. covers insured if driving another vehicle with permission

        d. pays legal fee if sued

        e. 50/100/10

            50 - amount for injuries to one person in one accident

            100 - maximum for injuries to 2 or more people

            10 - maximum for property damage

        f. 100/300/100 typically the maximum

        g. required by most states

    2. medical payment insurance

        a. covers auto accident medical expenses

        b. may duplicate coverage under your health insurance

    3. uninsured/underinsured motorists insurance

        a. inexpensive

        b. have it whether or not your state requires it

    4. collision insurance

        a. subject to a deductible

        b. covers only cost of repairing your car

        c. not mandatory unless car is financed

        d. blue book value - depreciated value

    5. comprehensive physical damage insurance

        a. covers car if stolen or damaged by vandalism, earthquake, flood, deer

        b. not mandatory unless car is financed

B. Financial responsibility and compulsory liability laws

  1. all states have financial responsibility laws which require drivers to show proof of ability to pay for accidents

  2. most states have compulsory liability insurance laws which require a minimum amount of bodily injury and property damage liability

C. No-fault insurance

  1. reduces the need to assign blame

  2. reduces time to get payment for damages

  3. reduces legal fees associated with accidents

  4. may deny right to have case heard in court

D. Auto insurance premiums

  1. amount and type of coverage

  2. place of residence

  3. personal characteristics

  4. automobile usage

  5. driving record

  6. type of car driven

V. Making The Right Auto Insurance Decision

A. Evaluating your existing insurance coverage

B. Saving money on auto insurance

  1. driving training

  2. good student

  3. multicar

  4. passive restraints

  5. multiple policies

C. Filing a claim

  1. call police

  2. ask for copy of police report

  3. protect your car from further damage

  4. take notes about accident and people involved

  5. notify your insurance company

  6. keep accurate records of expenses

  7. keep all paperwork related to the situation

Name _____   Instructor _____

Date _____   Section _____

Key Terminology Exercise - Fill In

1. Insurance companies are required to insure high risk drivers through the
   _____.

2. The best way to be sure that you will be able to rebuild your home if it is totally destroyed
   is to have _____ coverage.

3. To fully insure your rare coin collection you would need a(n) _____
   which is a(n) _____ to your regular homeowners policy.

4. What fathers do not want to hear their sons say is that the current condition of the family
   car is _____.

5. You have a(n) _____ to your friend if she falls down your basement steps
   because of your _____ in leaving a roller skate on the step.

6. Parents can be sued for the acts of their children because of _____ laws.

7. Hurricanes are a(n) _____ that you can avoid by moving to Iowa.

8. _____ was designed to reduce litigation and speed up settlements in auto
   accidents, but the effectiveness is controversial.

9. Failure to replace a light bulb on a dark stairway in your home is a lack of
   _____.

10. By increasing your _____ you can, in some cases, significantly reduce
    your homeowners insurance premiums.

11. In most states you can not purchase license plates without proof of insurance because of
    the _____ laws.

12. If you have an accident, the _____ may require that you put money in
    escrow to cover the damaged you caused.

13. If your short-wave radio antenna falls during a wind storm and damages your neighbor's
    home you may be financially responsible under the doctrine of _____.

Name _____   Instructor _____

Date _____   Section _____

Multiple Choice Questions

1. Homeowners insurance will cover personal property if it is stolen from
    a. your house.
    b. your garage.
    c. your motel room.
    d. all of the above

2. Of every 100 automobile accidents, the number caused by uninsured drivers is
    a. 8.
    b. 13.
    c. 21.
    d. 28.

3. In the event of a major disaster, like Hurricane Andrew, your homeowners insurance
    a. may not pay off at all if the insurance company goes under.
    b. will at least rebuild your home to current code requirements.
    c. may take months to settle your claim.
    d. a and c, only

4. If you own a home, you run the risk that
    a. a tornado will totally destroy it.
    b. a tornado will take off the roof making the house unlivable.
    c. someone will fall off your porch.
    d. all of the above

5. All of the following are examples of reasonable care for a public sidewalk **<u>except</u>**
    a. keeping it in good repair.
    b. putting in special lighting to supplement the already existing city street light.
    c. keeping the snow shoveled.
    d. putting salt on it when icy.

6. In a recent two year period there were over 1,500 liability cases in which the jury awarded damages in excess of
    a. 1 million dollars.
    b. 5 million dollars.
    c. 10 million dollars.
    d. 50 million dollars.

7. To get necessary excess personal liability protection you should purchase a(n)
    a. comprehensive insurance plan.
    b. umbrella policy.
    c. all-risk liability policy.
    d. homeowners and automobile insurance.

8. You should have excess personal liability protection if you
    a. are poor and have few assets.
    b. have a maid.
    c. work at home.
    d. b and c, only

9. If a visitor to your home is injured by tripping over a child's toy left in a dark hallway, your homeowners policy will cover this under
    a. personal property losses.
    b. liability.
    c. no-fault medical payments and damages.
    d. it is not covered by your homeowner's policy

10. If a visitor to your home is injured when a storm causes a tree limb to break off and crash through a window, your homeowners policy will cover this under
    a. personal property losses.
    b. liability.
    c. no-fault medical payments and damages.
    d. damages by trees and shrubs.

11. The broadest protection for the home owner can be obtained with a
    a. HO-3.
    b. HO-2.
    c. HO-1.
    d. a combination of all of the above.

12. Homeowners policy stipulates that you must carry insurance that, in relationship to the current replacement value of your home, is
    a. 100%.
    b. 80%.
    c. 60%.
    d. 40%.

13. As a renter you need insurance on
    a. your household contents and personal belongings.
    b. improvements to the building that you paid for.
    c. additional living expenses.
    d. all of the above

14. You should insure your home for
    a. what you paid for it.
    b. what you paid for it plus the cost of improvement.
    c. what it would cost today to rebuild it.
    d. what you could sell it for.

15. Flood insurance is
    a. available to only some homeowners.
    b. available to all homeowners.
    c. is seldom a good financial option.
    d. is always very expensive.

16. If your home is damaged, you should do all of the following **except**
    a. call you insurer immediately.
    b. do nothing to the house until an adjuster arrives.
    c. prepare a list of damaged or destroyed property.
    d. keep receipts for the meals you must eat at restaurants because your kitchen is unusable.

17. The bodily injury and property damage insurance will cover all of the following **except**
    a. hospital bills for someone struck by your car.
    b. repairs to a car struck by your car.
    c. repairs to your car.
    d. hospital bills for someone riding in your car.

18. In 42 states you are required to carry a minimum amount of
    a. liability insurance.
    b. comprehensive insurance.
    c. collision insurance.
    d. uninsured motorist insurance.

19. If your car's blue book value is under $2,000, you should consider dropping your
    a. collision coverage.
    b. comprehensive coverage.
    c. uninsured motorist coverage.
    d. a and b, only

20. All states require
    a. that you show proof of ability to pay accident-related damages.
    b. that you carry a minimum amount of liability insurance.
    c. escrow sufficient funds to cover accident-related damages.
    d. none of the above

21. No fault insurance
    a. results in lower premiums in the states that have it.
    b. eliminated fault as a factor in all cases.
    c. may deny you your day in court.
    d. has been unchanged in those states that have adopted it.

22. Your car insurance rates may be affected by
    a. where you live.
    b. your sex.
    c. your age.
    d. all of the above

Name _____   Instructor _____

Date _____   Section _____

Experiential Problems

1. A car is stolen every 20 seconds in this country. To lessen the chances that this may happen to you, fill out the safety check list below which was developed from the "Advice from the Experts" box in your text. Carry this check list with you in your car and review items 1 to 13 each time you leave your car. Do this until it becomes automatic. Check off items when they have been dealt with.

Car Theft Avoidance Check List

<u>Action</u>   <u>Checked</u>

1. Remove keys when not in car.   __

2. Keep doors locked at <u>all</u> times.   __

3. Keep windows up when not in car.   __

4. Park only in well lit areas.   __

5. Avoid parking in lonely isolated areas.   __

6. Remove all valuables when not in car.   __

7. Park in garage.   __

8. Keep garage locked.   __

9. Turn wheels sharply when parking car.   __

10. Engage emergency brake.   __

11. Carry registration and license on your
    person.   __

12. Anything in car with name and address is
    removed.   __

13. Activate anti theft device.   __

<u>Action</u>   <u>Date Completed</u>

14. If you have T-shaped door locks replace
    them with straight ones.   _____

15. Etch the vehicle identification number
    (VIN) in hard-to-find places in the car -   _____
    locations:

16. Install anti-theft device   _____

    (Club, alarm)

17. Prepare cards to keep on person and at
    home with the following information: _____

        make of car

        model

        year

        color

        license plate #

        VIN

2. Are you getting the most for your car insurance dollar? Complete the chart below. Using your current policy fill in the liability limits for your current coverage Under Company A, list the premiums you currently pay. For Company B, get quotes from an independent agent. For Company C, select a well known automobile insurance company. Compare the totals amounts.

		COMPANY		
COVERAGE	LIABILITY LIMITS	A	B	C

Bodily Injury	$ /person $ /occ*			
Property Damage	$ /occ*			
Uninsured Motorist	$ /person $ /occ*			
Personal Injury	$____ deductible			
Personal Property	$____ deductible			
Comprehensive				
Collision				
Discounts				
TOTALS		_____	_____	_____

*Abbreviation for occurance

3. Do you know what you have in your home and how much it would cost to replace? The following test will help to answer this question:

   Pick a room in your home and list on the next page what you think is in the room and the cost to replace it. Do this without doing a walk-through of the room. After you complete your list, do a thorough inspection of the room, listing those items that you did not include on your first list. Also list the estimated replacement cost of these items.

   When you have completed your inventory confirm your estimated replacement cost by calling or visiting stores to get the replacement cost. Enter the actual replacement cost in the appropriate column. Total both columns.

   What is the answer to the question asked above? Do you need to do a complete room-by-room inventory?

Item	Your estimated replacement cost	Actual replacement cost

Chapter 12 Solutions

What Do You Know?

1. F	6. F
2. F	7. F
3. T	8. F
4. F	9. T
5. F	10. T

Key Terminology Exercise - Fill In

1. assigned risk pool
2. full replacement cost
3. floater, endorsement
4. totaled
5. liability, negligence
6. vicarious liability
7. peril
8. No-fault insurance
9. reasonable care
10. deductible
11. compulsory liability insurance
12. financial responsibility laws
13. strict liability

Multiple Choice Questions

1. d	11. a
2. b	12. b
3. d	13. d
4. d	14. c
5. b	15. a
6. a	16. b
7. b	17. c
8. d	18. a
9. b	19. d
10. c	20. a
	21. c
	22. d

Part 5

Investments

Chapter 13

The Investment Decision

What Do You Know?

T F 1. I will probably work for one company until retirement and collect that company pension.

T F 2. Most retired people can live quite comfortably on what they receive from Social Security.

T F 3. A person at age 25 who plans to retire at age 65 will need to save $1 million to have a decent, but not fancy, standard of living.

T F 4. It is more important to invest in the stock market than to have an emergency fund.

T F 5. I am overwhelmed and scared by the thought of investing in the stock market.

T F 6. I know that with the right amount of research and a few good tips, I'll be able to find investments that produce a high return with very little, if any, risk.

T F 7. The phrase "don't put all your eggs in one basket" doesn't apply to investing because you may find one or two great investments and should put all your money there.

T F 8. It is a good and safe idea to put most of your savings into your company's employee stock purchase plan.

T F 9. Banks are a sound choice for your retirement fund.

T F 10. An investment is expected to make money over time, so some people consider fine art works to be an investment.

Chapter 13

The Investment Decision

Chapter Overview

If you grew up in a family where money was kept only in a bank, and retirement income was derived solely from Social Security and maybe a company pension, you may be thinking ''should I invest?''

Today, that is the wrong question. If you plan to purchase a house, retire in some degree of comfort, have a family, or improve your standard of living, the question becomes ''How can I make the best investment decisions for me?''

Investments can mean different things to different people but most invest in stocks, bonds, or money market instruments. Before you make a selection, you'll need to assess your risk tolerance. In other words, how much chance or uncertainty can you handle and still be able to sleep at night? It's a tough question to answer particularly once you know that the more risk you can handle the greater the return or the odds of making more money.

Chapter Outline

I. Why Invest

   A. Reasons

      1. to increase future wealth

      2. to supplement current income

      3. to reduce tax liability

      4. to make a major purchase, e.g., car, education, house

      5. to retire

      6. for fun

   B. The importance of investment decisions

      1. we live longer - need more retirement income

      2. flat growth in personal income

      3. changing labor market

      4. trend toward self-directed retirement plans

II. The Steps in the Investment Decision

    A. Setting investment goals

        1. why are you investing

        2. what do you want your investments to accomplish

        3. what kind of time frame do you have

        4. goals influenced by current income

    B. Risk and return assessment

        1. how long do you plan to invest

        2. what return do you expect

        3. how much risk can you handle

    C. Investment selection

        1. stocks - company ownership

        2. bonds - money lending

        3. money market instruments - money lending

    D. Investment management

        1. passive approach - buy and hold philosophy

        2. active approach - buy and sell philosophy

III. Understanding Risk and Return

    A. Sources of investment returns

        1. income
        2. price changes

    B. Measuring investment returns

        1. total returns

        2. average annual returns

    C. What is investment risk

        1. measuring investment risk

        2. are risk and holding period related?

    D. Comparing stocks, bonds, and T-bills

        1. total return - stocks

        2. stability of principal - T-bills

        3. current income - bonds

        4. stability of income - bonds

        5. growth of income - stocks

IV. Some Lessons for New Investors

    A. Positive relationship between risk and return

    B. Diversification is beneficial

    C. The past is not necessarily the future

        1. bull market - rising

        2. bear market - falling

    D. Financial markets function pretty well

    E. Avoiding common investment mistakes

        1. chasing returns

        2. investing in fads

        3. hanging on to a loser

        4. investing with no plan

        5. trusting the self-proclaimed gurus

        6. fearing the wrong risks

V. Sources of Investment Information

    A. Periodicals and newspapers

    B. Investment advisory services

        1. Moody's and Standard & Poor's

        2. Value Line

        3. Morningstar

        4. brokerage firms

        5. investment newsletters

    C. Computerized sources of investment information

Name _____   Instructor _____

Date _____   Section _____

Key Terminology Exercise- Matching

Match the words in column A to the statements in column B.

Column A

A. Expected return

B. Stocks

C. Bond

D. Face value

E. Money market instrument

F. Buy and hold

G. Transactions costs

H. Total return

I. Investment risk

J. Diversification

K. Bull market

L. Bear market

M. Financial markets

N. Objective source

O. Subjective source

Column B

___ 1. This is found by dividing the dividends received per share for a year and the amount of per share price increase by the original purchase price per share.

___ 2. No matter what you chose to invest in, you cannot <u>totally</u> avoid this.

___ 3. If you purchase a 20 year, $1000 bond - this is what the $1000 you will receive in 20 years is called.

___ 4. Value Line and *Fortune* are examples of this kind of information.

___ 5. The financial page of local newspapers that gives stock prices is an example of this kind of information.

___ 6. What you hope to earn on an investment in the coming year.

___ 7. If you do not have the time to review and make changes to your investment you should follow this approach to investing.

___ 8. If the money you are investing will be needed in a year or less, one of these is probably your best alternative.

___ 9. October 1929 saw the beginning of a long one of these.

___ 10. Discount brokers will help you keep these low if you wish to actively manage your investments.

___ 11. Investing all of your money in the stock of one company fails to achieve this objective of investing.

___ 12. To become the part owner of a company and share in the company's profits you must purchase this.

___ 13. If you purchase what is described in question 12, you hope that it will be followed by this kind of a market.

___ 14. The Over-the-Counter and AMEX are examples of this.

___ 15. This kind of investment is favored by older investors and gives you a fixed dollar payment each year for a set number of years.

Name _____   Instructor _____

Date _____   Section _____

Multiple Choice Questions

1. A common mistake made by investors is to under invest in
    a. T-bills.
    b. common stocks.
    c. bonds.
    d. CDs.

2. People invest in order to
    a. reduce the taxes they pay.
    b. buy a house.
    c. pay for college.
    d. all of the above

3. Some experts estimate that someone starting a career today will need to save for retirement
    a. $100,000
    b. $500,000
    c. $750,000
    d. over $1,000,000

4. Investing decisions today are more important than ever for all of the following reasons **except**
    a. we will spend our entire career with one company and therefore have only one pension to retire on.
    b. we will live longer after retirement and therefore need more money.
    c. personal incomes will grow much slower so we will need to save for big future purchases, not pay for them from our raises.
    d. more companies are using self-directed retirement plans where we must make most, if not all, of the investment decisions.

5. Most experts agree that before you can become an investor you must first be a
    a. debtor.
    b. saver.
    c. college graduate.
    d. family person.

6. One of the best first investments for many people is to
   a. open a savings account.
   b. buy a Series EE savings bond.
   c. pay off expensive credit card debt.
   d. buy gold coins.

7. You can make regular monthly investments to a mutual fund for as low as
   a. $1,000.
   b. $500.
   c. $100.
   d. $50.

8. For a 22 yearold college graduate, which of the following would **probably** **not** be a realistic financial goal?
   a. retire at age 55 with a $1,000,000 investment fund
   b. put two children through college
   c. save enough money while in college to pay cash for a Porsche
   d. own a home free and clear by age 45

9. Compared to stocks, bonds generally produce
   a. lower returns at lower risk.
   b. lower returns at high risk.
   c. higher returns at lower risk.
   d. higher returns at higher risk.

10. If you are currently putting $100 a month in a savings account at 3%, in order to have $1,000,000 for your retirement in 30 years you will need to
    a. increase your monthly savings.
    b. increase your return.
    c. increase your risk.
    d. all of the above

11. The longer your holding period for an investment
    a. the more risk you can take.
    b. the less risk you can take.
    c. the higher will be your guaranteed return.
    d. the lower will be your guaranteed return.

12. If you buy stock in a company you get all of the following **except**
    a. part ownership in the company.
    b. interest on your investment.
    c. potential increases in the price of the stock.
    d. a share in the profits in the form of cash dividends.

13. When you buy a bond you get all of the following **except**
    a. interest on your investment.
    b. the face value of the bond at maturity.
    c. an increase in the bond's price if interest rates fall.
    d. a share of the company's profits.

14. All of the following are true of money market instruments **except**
    a. you receive a pre-determined amount of interest.
    b. you get the face value at maturity.
    c. they mature in one year or more.
    d. you are lending money just like a bond.

15. A passive approach requires the investor to
    a. incur high transaction costs.
    b. make changes when personal goals change.
    c. frequently buy and sell.
    d. devote considerable time to their investments.

16. If an investor wishes to get the maximum percentage return on an investment, the investor will need to
    a. invest for a shorter period of time.
    b. invest more money.
    c. accept more risk.
    d. all of the above

17. Through the diversification of investments an investor may
    a. reduce risk and increase return.
    b. reduce risk and not substantially reduce return.
    c. increase risk and return.
    d. increase risk and substantially reduce return.

18. A good rule to follow with regards to your investments is to
    a. buy what was hot last year.
    b. admit your mistakes, sell them, and move on.
    c. just get started and work out a plan as you learn.
    d. get a book on investing and do what it says.

Name _____   Instructor _____

Date _____   Section _____

Experiential Problems

1. One of the keys to being a successful investor is the proper matching of investment instruments to the investor's risk tolerance. Some individuals have a very high risk tolerance and enjoy such things as bungy jumping. Others find a walk in the park about as risky as they want to be.

    As a first step in your investing career you need to determine your own risk tolerance so that you can plan an investing program that will work for you. This self-test is designed to do just that, evaluate your individual risk tolerance. After you have taken and graded it, use the results to assist you in your financial planning in not just this course, but throughout the rest of your life.

    As a person's risk tolerance may change somewhat over time you may wish to keep this test in your financial records and retake it periodically as part of your regular review of your investment goals and strategies. You may also want to take other risk tolerance tests published in magazines from time to time or made available by brokerage firms and compare the results to get the best overall feel for your risk tolerance.

Risk Tolerance Test

Indicate in the space provided true (T) or false (F) as the statement applies to you. Do not read the answer key before taking the test.

_____ 1. If I have misplaced my wallet I cannot go to bed until I find it.

_____ 2. I need to see a very specific list of my duties and responsibilities before I can accept a job.

_____ 3. I would never loan money to friends or family members.

_____ 4. I do not enjoy the thought of moving to a new city or town.

_____ 5. I like to have my day planned out, even weekends.

_____ 6. If I bought stock I would check the price daily.

_____ 7. I have had no more than one speeding ticket in the last two years.

_____ 8. I would not have unprotected sex with anyone, except a spouse, no matter how long I had known them.

_____ 9. I can not understand why people do things like sky diving, bungy jumping and white water rafting.

_____ 10. I never cook with a crock pot or self-timing oven when I am not at home.

2. To get you on the road to investing you need to have an clear idea of just how ready you are.

a. Complete the chart, derived from Exhibit 13.1 in your text, to determine how ready you are to begin investing. If you have six "yes" responses in column 2, you are ready.

Activity	Completed* (yes or no)	Do you have a completion date? -enter date if "yes"
1. Set short and long run personal goals		
2. Prepare current financial statements		
3. Develop and follow a realistic budget		
4. Establish a regular savings program		
5. Manage credit properly		
6. Have adequate and appropriate insurance coverage		

*If you put a "yes" in this column, the remainder of the columns on this line will be blank.

b. For any activity for which you gave two "no" answers, you need to develop an action plan. In the space provided, develop the necessary action plans to accomplish the activities that will prepare you to begin investing.

In developing your action plans, be sure to answer the following questions.

(1) What must I accomplish? (Example - pay off credit card debts of $xxx.)

(2) How will I accomplish it? (Example - cut up credit cards, reduce spending to free-up funds for debt repayment.)

(3) Who or where will I go to seek help - if necessary? (Example - to my bank since they provide free credit counseling services to their depositors.)

(4) When can I accomplish this activity? (Example - by reducing certain expenditures my revised budget shows $xx available for credit card payments which factoring in interest I can have the cards paid off by x-x-9x.)

Action Plans- continued

3. Now that you have determined your risk tolerance and readiness to begin investing, you need to identify those financial goals you have established in which investing can and should play a role.

   For some financial goals (paying off credit cards or obtaining adequate insurance) investing plays no or a limited role. Other financial goals (retiring at age 50 or sending your children to college) can most easily be reached by skillful investing.

   It is also important to understand the risk tolerance of your goals. Goals have two aspects of risk tolerance that should be addressed. The first deals with the time horizon of the goal and the second revolves around the consequences of not achieving it.

   An example would be your goal of purchasing a new car in four years. The time horizon is relatively short, so a low to moderate risk investment is called for. The consequence of not getting a new car is not life and death as there are alternatives - repair the old car, buy a used car or use public transportation - so a moderate level of risk may be acceptable.

   Another example would be to take a trip around the world at age 50 (current age 25). The time horizon is long, so high risk can be tolerated. The consequence of not taking the trip is only disappointment so here again high risk can be accepted.

   Fill out the chart, but leave out the last column ''Best suited investment instrument'' until you have completed chapter 15. experiential problem #1 in chapter 15 will refer you back to the chart for completion.

Financial Goal	Time Horizon* Risk Tolerance*	Achievement Risk Tolerance*	Best Suited Investment Instrument

Chapter 13 Solutions

What Do You Know?

1. F	6. F
2. F	7. F
3. T	8. F
4. F	9. F
5. F	10. T

Key Terminology Exercise - Matching

1. H	6. A	11. J
2. I	7. F	12. B
3. D	8. E	13. K
4. O	9. L	14. M
5. N	10. G	15. C

Multiple Choice

1. b	11. a
2. d	12. b
3. d	13. d
4. a	14. c
5. b	15. b
6. c	16. c
7. d	17. b
8. c	18. b
9. a	
10. d	

Experiential Problems

1.

Grading for Risk Tolerance Test

Number of answers marked T	Risk tolerance category	Possible investments that you will feel comfortable with
10-9	Conservative	Investment grade bonds, T-bills, notes, bonds
8-7	Moderately Conservative	Investment grade bonds, T-bills, notes, bonds, some blue chip stocks
6-5	Conservative Growth	Some fixed income securities, blue chip stocks, growth stocks
4-3	Moderately Aggressive	Growth stock, international stocks, some small cap or ''penny'' stocks
2-1	Aggressive	Nearly all aggressive growth stocks, small cap and international stock
0	Wild thing	Exotic-options, futures, collectibles, real estate, you name it!!

Chapter 14

Investment Alternatives and Trading

What Do You Know?

T F 1. I don't know anyone who owns stocks.

T F 2. I have heard the term "mutual funds."

T F 3. I don't have enough money to invest.

T F 4. Real estate is typically a safer investment than any kind of stocks.

T F 5. I'll think about investing when I'm older.

T F 6. Bonds are good investments for anyone.

T F 7. The best way to pick stocks is to research the company thoroughly.

T F 8. The best way to make money in the stock market is to watch the prices daily then buy and sell quickly, called timing the market.

T F 9. It is silly to select stocks based on products/services you like and use.

T F 10. Life insurance is the best investment.

Chapter 14

Investment Alternatives and Trading

Chapter Overview

Investing can be a confusing and overwhelming venture, particularly if the image in your mind is that of the frenzied activity on the floor of the New York Stock Exchange. This chapter divides today's investment alternatives into categories, explaining key terms and characteristics within each category. Stocks and bonds comprise the bulk of the chapter and provide a critical understanding on which to build the information of the future chapters. Knowing where and how to get investment advice is critical, and you'll learn tips and warnings for selecting a broker.

Chapter Outline

I.   Classifying Today's Investment Alternatives

   A. 50,000 investment alternatives

   B. direct investments - actual ownership, e.g., T-bills or stocks

   C. indirect investments - own shares of an investment company which actually owns the investment, e.g., mutual funds

II. Fixed Incomes Securities

   A. You are lending money in exchange for a fixed amount of interest

   B. Prime reason to buy is for income

   C. All mature or grow to a fixed amount known at time of sale

   D. You have certain legal rights should you not get your money

   E. Money market instruments

      1. sold for less than face value

      2. little or no risk

      3. sold with large face value

      4. money market mutual funds or T-bills

   F. Bonds (long-term fixed income)

      1. maturity in excess of one year

      2. regular fixed amount of interest

3. callable - issuer may buy back

4. wide variance in terms of risk

G. Treasury notes and bonds

1. treasury notes - maturities of 2, 3, 5, 10 years and not callable

2. treasury bonds - maturities of 30 years and callable 5 years prior to maturity

3. both have fixed coupon rates and face values of $1,000 - $5,000

4. no risk

5. interest is exempt from state tax

H. Municipal bonds

1. issued by governmental units

2. revenue bonds - pay for a project and backed by the project revenues

3. general obligation bonds - backed by the state where the bonds were issued

4. interest exempt from federal income taxes

5. some risk, so bonds are rated from AAA - D

I. Corporate bonds

1. mortgage bond - (asset-backed bond) backed up by equipment or real estate

2. debenture - most common, less risky than #1, backed by general credit of the company

3. floating rate - similar to adjustable rate mortgage

4. pre-refunded bond - repayment guaranteed by another bond

5. subordinated debenture - more risk than ordinary debentures and pay higher coupon rates

6. zero coupon bond - sell for deep discounts and price rises as maturity approaches

J. Mortgage pass-through securities

1. fixed number of mortgages with same interest rate and term

2. like a mutual fund of mortgages

3. low risk

4. uncertain maturity

K. What determines bond prices

1. cash interest payments you receive

2. length of time you receive these payments

3. interest rate used to discount these payments (yield-to-maturity)

III. Stock Investing

   A. Why invest in common stock

      1. dividends

      2. increase in stock price

   B. Types of common stock

      1. blue chip stocks - long records of stable earnings and dividend growth

      2. growth stocks - rapid sales and earnings growth to continue

      3. income stocks - slow price appreciation and dividend increases with lower risk

      4. speculative stocks - gamble on new information

      5. cyclical vs. defensive stocks - relationship between stock prices and business cycle

   C. Valuing common stocks

      1. profits or current level of earnings

      2. current level of dividends

      3. expected growth rate of earnings and dividends

      4. uncertainty over growth rate in earnings and dividends

      5. level of interest rates

   D. Some important numbers

      1. return on equity equals sales minus expenses divided by shareholders' equity

      2. earnings per share equals sales minus expenses divided by outstanding shares

      3. price-earnings ratio equals current stock price divided by current annual earnings

      4. beta - risk of a stock relative to the overall market

IV. Beyond Stocks and Bonds

   A. Real estate

      1. risky

      2. requires large time commitment

      3. generally lower returns than stocks and bonds

   B. Exotic investments

      1. options and futures

      2. real assets

      3. collectibles

V. Understanding Financial Markets

    A. Characteristics of a good market

        1. trading occurs in full view of buyers and sellers

        2. sufficient availability of information

        3. can trade at a price close to a recent, similar trade

        4. equal access to the market

    B. Types of financial markets

        1. primary vs. secondary markets

        2. where trading takes place

    C. Examples of financial markets

        1. NYSE (Big Board)

        2. NASDAQ

    D. Buying and selling securities

        1. open a brokerage account

        2. fill out an account application

        3. meet the minimum amount of cash

    E. Selecting a brokerage firm and a broker

        1. full-service firms, e.g., Paine Weber, Merrill Lynch

        2. discount firm, e.g., Charles Schwab, Quick & Reilly

        3. should belong to SIPC

        4. selecting a broker

            a. paid on commission

            b. should complete a financial history with goals, time frames, risk tolerance, etc.

            c. should explain commissions and fees

            d. should explain rate of return computations

    F. Types of orders and trades

        1. market order

            a. most common

            b. payment due within 3 days

        2. limit order

            a. sets a limit on price

            b. valid for a certain period of time

            c. higher commissions

G. Investment record keeping

1. tax purposes
2. track performance
3. monthly statements from brokerage firm
4. personal financial software programs
5. your own system
   a. description
   b. investment type
   c. reason for purchase
   d. cost basis
   e. annual income
   f. current market value
   g. change in value
   h. comments

Name _____   Instructor _____

Date _____   Section _____

Key Terminology Exercise - Fill In

1. Companies like AT & T whose stock price does not change significantly are still attractive to investors because of the _____ that it pays stockholders four times a year and are considered _____ .

2. Food Lion, a large southern grocery chain, is a _____ because its stock price does not directly respond to the business cycle.

3. Near the end of a recession a stock like GM is probably a good investment because it is a _____ and should go up in price as the economy recovers.

4. If you own a bond that is _____ and interest rates are falling there is a good chance you will not be allowed to hold the bond to maturity.

5. To obtain the highest return and also the highest risk of default from an investment in corporate bonds you would need to purchase _____ .

6. Any bond rated by Standard & Poor's in its top four categories (AAA, AA, A, and BBB) is considered to be of _____ .

7. The only sure way to receive the face value of a bond is to wait until it _____ .

8. One way to tell if a company is ''in trouble'' is the lowering of their _____ by Standard & Poor's indicating an increase in the _____ of the company's bonds.

9. GM, Xerox, Eastman Kodak, GE and AT&T are all companies whose stocks are considered _____ .

10. The Imperial Russian Government has failed to pay interest on their bonds since 1916, which puts them in _____ .

11. When the price of a bond changes it's _____ also changes but in the opposite direction.

Name _____   Instructor _____

Date _____   Section _____

Multiple Choice Questions

1. In the last ten years the number of Americans has doubled who own
    a. stocks.
    b. savings accounts.
    c. life insurance.
    d. a home.

2. In order to be an intelligent investor in today's market, you must understand
    a. the alternative investment.
    b. the workings of the financial markets.
    c. how investments are bought and sold.
    d. all of the above

3. An investor in today's market has a choice of investment alternatives that numbers close to
    a. 25,000.
    b. 50,000.
    c. 75,000.
    d. 100,000.

4. All of the following are examples of direct investments **except**
    a. stocks.
    b. bonds.
    c. mutual funds.
    d. antique cars.

5. Which of these is (are) indirect investments?
    a. options
    b. unit investment trusts
    c. mutual funds
    d. b and c, only

6. All of the following are true of money market instruments **except**
    a. they are sold at a discount.
    b. they have a high default risk.
    c. they are sold with large face values.
    d. All are true of money market instruments.

7. U.S. Treasury bills are
   a. sold at a discount.
   b. purchased only through brokerage firms.
   c. sold in face values as low as $10,000.
   d. a and c, only

8. All of the following are examples of bonds **except**
   a. notes.
   b. money market instruments.
   c. debentures.
   d. mortgage pass-through securities.

9. With a 6%, $5,000 bond you would receive how much interest every six months?
   a. $300
   b. $30
   c. $150
   d. $15

10. Treasury notes and bonds are the same, **except** that
    a. bonds have face values over $5,000 while notes are under $5,000.
    b. bonds are callable and notes generally are not.
    c. notes have longer maturities.
    d. notes are sold at a discount and bonds are not.

11. One of the following is not exempt form at least some income taxes.
    a. revenue bonds
    b. federal agency bonds
    c. mortgage pass-through securities
    d. general obligation bonds

12. A bond that is backed by the land and buildings of the corporation is a
    a. mortgage bond.
    b. debenture.
    c. floating rate bond.
    d. pre-funded bond.

13. On a bond, all of the following are fixed **except**
    a. the amount of each interest payment.
    b. the yield to maturity.
    c. the face value amount.
    d. dates payments will be received.

14. An individual who wishes to invest in a stock that will produce a reliable dividend payment on which the investor will live should buy a stock that is
    a. income and speculative.
    b. income and blue chip.
    c. income and growth.
    d. income and cyclical.

15. Stock prices are influenced by
    a. current earnings.
    b. past earnings.
    c. future earnings.
    d. a and c, only

16. A company's beta is 2 and the market rises by 10%. The company's stock price should
    a. rise by 20%.
    b. rise by 10%.
    c. fall by 10%.
    d. fall by 20%.

17. The price-earnings ratio is found by dividing the stock price by
    a. return on equity.
    b. yield to maturity.
    c. project earnings.
    d. current earnings.

18. Which of the following as a group is generally the most risky?
    a. stocks
    b. bonds
    c. mutual funds
    d. collectibles

19. The New York Stock Exchange is an example of a(n)
    a. primary market.
    b. secondary market.
    c. over-the-counter market.
    d. a and c, only

20. The NASDAQ is an example of a
    a. primary market.
    b. secondary market.
    c. over-the-counter market.
    d. b and c, only

21. You own a stock that has gone up in price. You think it may go up more but you do not wish to lose the profit you have already made. Which of the following will be of use to you?

    a. market order

    b. limit order

    c. specialists order

    d. none of the above

Name _____   Instructor _____

Date _____   Section _____

Experiential Problems

1. We live in an age of information that at times is overwhelming. Successful investors identify a usable number of information sources and for the most part ignore the rest. You need to identify the sources of information that will best meet your needs and use them. Over the next week or two acquaint yourself with the sources of financial information available to you. You may get some ideas for the five stocks you will need for experiential problem #2.

   Your personal schedule and investment needs (active vs. passive investor just to mention one factor) will dictate the sources most suitable to you. A busy lifestyle may make taped segments from CNBC that can be viewed at night your best choice. A very active investor may have need of the <u>Wall Street Journal</u> or <u>Investor's Business Daily</u> for daily input to investment decisions.

   As you acquaint yourself with the available information sources, ask yourself the following questions.

   a. What is the target market of this source - is it directed to the small investor or large corporate ones?

   b. What level of knowledge is needed to use the information - an MBA in finance or general knowledge?

   c. What does the information cost? (If you only have $100 a month to invest, an information source that cost $2,000 a year is not cost effective.)

   When you are finished, complete the table for the 3 to 5 sources you selected for your use.

Information source	Cost	Reason for selection
1.		
2.		
3.		
4.		
5.		

2. Good record keeping is a part of good investing. To practice this, pick five stocks that are listed daily in the <u>Wall Street Journal</u> or the financial pages of your local paper. Do not worry about matching them to your risk tolerance or financial goals.

    Using the worksheets provided, track the five stocks over the remainder of the semester updating your records every Friday. You may buy and sell as you wish. Assume you have $10,000 to invest. At the end of the term, just for fun, compute the value of your portfolio.

    How did you do? Remember, you did little or no research on your picks and did not diversify between bonds and stocks so do not worry if you lost money.

Exhibit 14.10
Investment Record Worksheet

Description	Type	Investment Objective	Annual Income	Cost Basis	Current Value	Percent Difference	Comments

Exhibit 14.10
Investment Record Worksheet

Description	Type	Investment Objective	Annual Income	Cost Basis	Current Value	Percent Difference	Comments

Exhibit 14.10
Investment Record Worksheet

Description	Type	Investment Objective	Annual Income	Cost Basis	Current Value	Percent Difference	Comments

Exhibit 14.10
Investment Record Worksheet

Description	Type	Investment Objective	Annual Income	Cost Basis	Current Value	Percent Difference	Comments

Exhibit 14.10
Investment Record Worksheet

Description	Type	Investment Objective	Annual Income	Cost Basis	Current Value	Percent Difference	Comments

Exhibit 14.10
Investment Record Worksheet

Description	Type	Investment Objective	Annual Income	Cost Basis	Current Value	Percent Difference	Comments

3. Selecting a broker is an important and challenging part of your investment program. One way to accomplish this task is to interview several prospective brokers as you would a prospective employee, except you will go to the broker's office to conduct the interview. The broker, after all, is supposed to be working for you to assist you in reaching your financial goals.

    To help you get started, talk to friends and family members for recommendations. Keep in mind, however, that a good broker for your parents may not be good for you. Try to interview at least three or four as your time allows. The more you interview, the better sense you will have of exactly what you are seeking in a good broker.

    The following list of questions is not all inclusive so feel free to add your own.

Interview questions for prospective brokers

1. How long have you been a broker?

2. How long have you been with this firm?

3. What degrees/training do you have?

4. How is your client base broken down?

    By age?

    % under 30?

    % 30 - 50?

    % over 50?

    By sex?

    % male?

    % female?

    By occupation?

    % white collar?

    % blue collar?

    Portfolio size?

    % under $100,000?

    % over $100,000?

    Average size? $_____

5. What do you need to know about a client before you can advise him/her on investments?

6. Explain your firm's fee structure on various kinds of investments.

7. Please review a sample statement that I will receive if I am a client. How can I compute a rate of return from this statement?

Some observations you should be making during the interview.

1. Is the broker taking time with me, showing an interest in my needs or is he/she trying to rush me out?

2. Is the broker talking down to me?

3. Is the broker using a lot of technical jargon to "snow" me or trying to be "user-friendly?"

4. Is the broker professional looking? Is this a person from appearances I would trust with my life savings?

5. Is the broker's office neat and orderly looking?

Chapter 14 Solutions

What Do You Know?

1.	F	6.	F
2.	T	7.	T
3.	F	8.	F
4.	F	9.	F
5.	F	10.	F

Key Terminology Exercise - Fill In

1. dividends, income stocks
2. defensive stock
3. cyclical stock
4. callable
5. junk bonds
6. investment grade
7. mature
8. bond ratings, default risk
9. blue chip
10. default
11. yield to maturity

Multiple Choice Questions

1.	a	11.	c
2.	e	12.	a
3.	b	13.	b
4.	c	14.	b
5.	d	15.	d
6.	b	16.	a**
7.	d	17.	d
8.	b	18.	d
9.	c*	19.	b
10.	b	20.	d
		21.	b

Calculations for Multiple Choice Questions:
* 9. ($5000 x .06/2 = $150)
**16. (10% x 2 = 20%)

Chapter 15

Investing in Mutual Funds

What Do You Know?

T F 1. Mutual funds are each an attractive and popular choice because people feel they are safer than direct ownership of stocks and bonds.

T F 2. Mutual funds are safer than stocks and bonds.

T F 3. Stocks and bonds earn better returns than mutual funds.

T F 4. You can start investing in mutual funds for relatively little money.

T F 5. I know people who own mutual funds.

T F 6. There are special advantages to mutual funds.

T F 7. Mutual funds are better for older investors.

T F 8. Mutual funds are good for the long term investor.

T F 9. Mutual funds only invest in stocks.

T F 10. You need to know more about investing to invest in stocks and bonds than in mutual funds.

Chapter 15

Investing in Mutual Funds

Chapter Overview

Mutual funds are a popular and attractive investment choice for many people of all ages and incomes. You can get started for as little as an initial $250 or a commitment to invest $50 a month. Mutual funds offer professional management in that one person is responsible for buying and selling the shares that made up the fund. This should be a person with the knowledge and background to do the job well. And finally, mutual funds offer diversification. There are over 7,000 funds so that one has to exist to match your risk tolerance, expected returns, and investment philosophy. And if you own several mutual funds, you have diversity within diversity!

Chapter Outline

I. Understanding Mutual Funds

    A. How a mutual fund operates

        1. organization which raises funds by selling shares to investors
        2. investor funds are used to purchase securities consistent with the objectives of the mutual fund
        3. also called open-end investment companies
        4. NAV - net asset value or current market value

    B. How to buy mutual fund shares

        1. through stockbroker or directly from fund
        2. obtain a prospectus and an application

    C. Services offered

        1. automatic reinvestment of distributions
        2. automatic investment plans
        3. exchange privileges
        4. check writing

    D. Regulation and taxation

        1. regulated by U.S. Securities and Exchange Commission

2. distributions - income and realized capital gains passed to shareholders, who, in turn, must report on their tax returns

E. Where to get mutual fund information

1. public and college libraries
2. Morningstar and CDA/Wiesenberger - mutual fund rating services
3. <u>Money</u> <u>Magazine</u>

F. Classifying mutual funds

1. stock funds
   a. aggressive growth
   b. growth and income
   c. long term growth
   d. small company growth
   e. international
   f. total return
2. bond funds
   a. government
   b. high yield corporate
   c. investment-grade corporate
   d. mortgage-backed securities
   e. municipal bond
   f. world income
3. money market funds
   a. government
   b. taxable
   c. tax-exempt
4. asset allocation funds
   a. total return funds
   b. mixture of stocks, bonds, and money market instruments
   c. high returns with less volatility
5. index funds
   a. replicate the performance of a major stock index
   b. average stock fund typically doesn't beat the overall stock market
   c. very low fees
6. sector funds
   a. specialized funds investing in one industry
   b. more risk
   c. not for new investors

II. Advantages of Mutual Funds

    A. Diversification

    B. Smaller minimum investments

    C. Professional management

III. Picking the Right Mutual Funds

    A. Establishing Investment Objectives

        1. establish your investment goals
        2. assess your risk tolerance and return expectations
        3. match the mutual fund with your goals, time frame, rate of return, and risk tolerance.

    B. What do mutual funds charge?

        1. load charges

            a. fees associated with buying or redeeming shares
            b. front-end load
                (1) can't exceed 8.5%
                (2) paid when shares are initially purchased
            c. no-load
            d. back-end load
                (1) contingent deferred sales charges (CDSCs)
                (2) paid when shares are redeemed
                (3) longer held, the lower the load
        2. annual operating expenses
        3. 12b-1 fees
        4. standardizing fees and expenses

    C. Evaluating fees and expenses

        1. substantial variation in fees
        2. higher fees and expenses can negatively impact the value of an investment over time
        3. no proof that fees and expenses relate in any way to performance
        4. start by buying funds with low operating expenses and no loads

    D. Historical performance

        1. total return - measures return over time including income and price changes
        2. relative performance - meaningful comparison to a standard make up of securities in which the fund invests
        3. risk
        4. overall rating

E. The relationship between past and future performance

 1. some believe past performance is a poor indicator of future performance

 2. others believe past performance is a reasonable predictor of future performance

F. Performance and taxes

 1. the higher the investment income and realized capital gains, the greater your tax liability

 2. never purchase a mutual fund right before it makes a cash contribution

E. Other considerations when choosing a fund

 1. manager's investment philosophy

 2. derivative contracts

 3. derivative securities

 4. big sector bets

 5. foreign securities

H. What about index funds?

IV. Managing Mutual Fund Investments

 A. Lump sum investing vs. dollar cost averaging

 1. dollar cost averaging - equal dollar amounts at regular intervals over a period of time

 2. requires discipline to make regular investments each month

 B. Making changes to your mutual fund investments

 1. as you move through the life cycle

 2. rebalancing - to put your portfolio back in line with your goals

 C. When to sell a mutual fund

 1. don't sell to chase returns

 2. don't make decisions based on short term performances

 3. warning signs include:

 a. sub-par performance for 3 consecutive years

 b. fund gets too large quickly

 c. steadily rising expenses

 d. management turnover

Name _____ Instructor _____

Date _____ Section _____

Key Terminology Exercise - Crossword Puzzle

Using the words found in the Running Glossary, complete the crossword puzzle. An X indicates a space between words in a multi-word answer. Clues to the puzzle are on the next page.

<u>Across</u>

1. Avoid buying mutual funds at least a month before one of these.

5. A potential investor will find all he or she needs to know about a mutual fund in which document?

7. The action that may be taken as a result of a careful analysis of your investments.

8. Another name for an indirect investment whose popularity has skyrocketed since 1980.

<u>Down</u>

1. An approach to investing over time instead of investing in a lump sum.

2. The Janus Fund and the Janus Mercury Fund are part of the Janus group which is called what?

3. By law there are limited to 8.5%, but may be 0.

4. The price you will pay to purchase shares in a mutual fund plus load charge, if any.

6. A fee paid to purchase a mutual fund payable at the time of purchase.

Name _____ Instructor _____

Date _____ Section _____

Multiple Choice Questions

1. The increase in the number of mutual funds since 1980 resulted from
   a. the historic bull market.
   b. the increase in investor knowledge.
   c. self-directed retirement plans.
   d. a and c, only

2. All of the following are true statements about mutual funds **except**
   a. they are open-end investment companies.
   b. they issue new shares directly to investors.
   c. they are listed on the New York Stock Exchange.
   d. interest and dividends received on fund investments are passed along to shareholders.

3. The net asset value of a mutual fund is found by dividing the total number of shares into what number less any liabilities?
   a. original cost of the securities owned by the fund
   b. current market value of the securities owned by the fund
   c. the total dividends and interest received ont he securities owned by the fund during the current year.
   d. none of the above

4. Before buying shares in a mutual fund you must
   a. obtain and read a prospectus.
   b. fill out an application.
   c. determine that the funds investment is consistent with your own.
   d. all of the above

5. Mutual funds may offer its shareholders all of the following services **except**
   a. advice on which of their funds best meets your investment needs.
   b. automatic reinvestment of distributions into the purchase of more shares.
   c. automatic deductions from your checking account to purchase shares.
   d. transfer of money from one fund to another within the same family of funds.

6. Mutual funds almost never pay income taxes because
   a. they only invest in tax exempt securities.
   b. they are exempt under IRS regulations.
   c. they pass along their earnings to their shareholders who pay the taxes.
   d. they seldom have earnings.

7. Mutual funds are classified by
   a. investment objectives.
   b. investment style.
   c. types of securities owned.
   d. a and c, only

8. Only one of the following is a true statement about mutual funds.
   a. The majority of mutual funds have their assets invested in stocks.
   b. An aggressive growth fund is a stock mutual fund.
   c. A total return fund is a bond fund.
   d. The performance of different stock mutuals in the same sub-category will be very similar to each other.

9. A stock mutual fund may have its assets invested in
   a. stocks.
   b. bonds.
   c. T-bills.
   d. all of the above

10. If you are only going to purchase one fund, some experts would recommend a(n)
    a. asset allocation fund.
    b. index fund.
    c. sector fund.
    d. any of the above

11. Stock mutual funds give investors the benefits of
    a. diversification.
    b. protection from bear markets.
    c. smaller minimum investments.
    d. a and c, only

12. The fee to purchase mutual funds may be
    a. paid at the time of purchase.
    b. paid at the time of sale.
    c. nonexistent.
    d. all of the above

13. Operating expenses for stock mutual funds as a percentage of assets are approximately
    a. 1.5%.
    b. 3.2%.
    c. 8.5%.
    d. over 11%.

14. In evaluating the cost of owning mutual funds, you must understand that
    a. operating expenses of mutual funds vary substantially from fund to fund.
    b. fees and expenses can have an impact on the value of your investment.
    c. there is a relationship between fees or load charges and performance.
    d. all of the above

15. Dollar cost averaging is not effective if the price of the investment
    a. falls consistently.
    b. moves erratically up and down.
    c. rises consistently.
    d. remains stable.

16. It is suggested by experts that the following warning sign(s) be watched for.
    a. failure to outperform benchmarks in any given year
    b. rising expenses
    c. management turnover
    d. b and c, only

Name _____   Instructor _____

Date _____   Section _____

Experiential Problems

1. Understanding the relationship of risk among investment instruments will help you to better plan your own investment strategy. You have now studied the various investment instruments listed below. They are listed in no particular order.

Investment Instruments

money market instruments

T-bills

T-notes

T-bonds

municipal bonds (various ratings)

corporate bonds (various ratings)

mortgage pass-through securities

common stocks:	blue chip
	growth
	income
	speculative
	cyclical
	defensive
exotic investments:	options and futures
	real estate
	collectibles
mutual funds:	asset allocation
	index
	sector

a. Use the worksheet on the next page to rank the risk of investment instruments. Arrange the investment instruments in order from least risky to most risky based on what you have learned or know about them. You may consider some of equal risk, so list them on the same line.

b. Our views are often influenced or biassed by our environment, family or other influences in our lives. For example, you may have heard stories from grandparents about how they knew people who lost everything in the stock market crash of 1929. This could color your view of common stocks as more risky than the recent facts might otherwise indicate. Review your list carefully and think of why you ranked the instruments the way you did. Be honest. Were any of the rankings influenced by bias not supportable by facts? Briefly note your reasons for ranking each as you did. For example if you listed T-bills at the top of the list, your reasons may have been: short term, what could happen to the government in just six months?

C. Now that you have determined your own risk tolerance (experiential problem 1 in chapter 13), the risk tolerance of your financial goals (experiential problem 3 in chapter 13) and the relative risk of the available investment instruments you are ready to complete the last column "Best suited investment instruments" on the chart in experiential problem 3 in chapter 13. Fill in the column by listing the investment instruments that you feel will best help you achieve your financial goals.

Worksheet
Risk Ranking of Investment Instruments

Investment Instruments	Risk Ranking	Reason for Ranking

2. With over 7,000 mutual funds to chose from, investors need to have a means of narrowing this 7,000 down to a workable number of options. This experiential problem is designed to help you identify the kind of fund that will help meet your financial goals. It will <u>not</u> help to identify the specific fund.

   a. Answer the following questions about your financial goals. Circle the answer that is truest of your financial goals.

      1. The time horizons of my goals is

under 2 years	2 to 5 years	5 to 10 years	10+ years

      2. As to principal, I need

stability	preservation	some growth	maximum growth

      3. Income is important.

yes	no

      4. Liquidity is important.

yes	no	somewhat

    Using your answers as the basis for an investor profile, compare them to the profiles given on the following pages to determine the kinds of mutual funds that should best suit your needs.

Investor Profiles

Current Income

Goal: *Higher current income than money market funds and liquidity*

Mutual Fund Mix:

This portfolio consists primarily of short-term and intermediate-term bond funds. These investments generally earn higher income than money market instruments or certificates of deposits while emphasizing safety and stability.

Appropriate for investors with the following profile:

Investors with short-term goals.

Those seeking stability of principal.

Those who want higher current income than money market investments, but who understand that principal will fluctuate.

Those who need to keep their account liquid.

Asset Mix: 100% Fixed Income

Kinds of funds: Corporate Bond, Money Market

Capital Preservation

Goal: *Stability of principal and protection from inflation*

Mutual Fund Mix:

This portfolio's goal is to safeguard principal, or the amount of money you invest. To do so, it is invested primarily in corporate and government bond funds for income, with relative stability in the price of fund shares. The portfolio also contains a small stock component which provides some potential for growth.

Appropriate for investors with the following profile:

Investors with short to intermediate time horizions, (2 to 5 years).

Those who are primarily interested in protecting their investment.

Those who want some growth as a hedge against inflation.

Asset Mix: 75% Fixed Income/25% Equity

Kinds of Funds: Corporate Bond, Equity Value, Equity Income

Investor Profiles

Moderate Growth

Goal: *Balanced growth and current income*

Mutual Fund Mix:

The strong commitment to bond funds provides some current income and helps stabilize the portfolio from inordinate swings in value.

Appropriate for investors with the following profile:

> Investors with intermediate goals (5 to 10 years).
>
> Those seeking more stability in "up" and "down" markets than stocks alone provide.
>
> Those seeking moderate current income.
>
> Investors who want to build capital and protect the value of their portfolio while avoiding inordinate swings in portfolio value.

Asset Mix: 60% Fixed Income/40% Equity

Kinds of funds: Corporate Bond, Equity Value, Equity Growth, Equity Income

---

Wealth Building

Goal: *Long -term Growth*

Mutual Fund Mix:

This portfolio is invested in a diversified mix of stock and bond funds to build assets and protect against inflation over the long run.

Appropriate for investors with the following profile:

> Investors with long-term goals, (10+ years).
>
> Those who are more interested in beating inflation.
>
> Those less concerned with short term fluctuations.
>
> Investors seeking a diversified approach to wealth accumulation.

Asset Mix: 35% Fixed Income/65% Equity

Kinds of Funds: Corporate Bond, Equity Value, Equity Growth, Equity Income, Equity Small Cap

Investor Profiles

Aggressive Appreciation

Goal: *Maximum growth of principal*

Mutual Fund Mix:

To provide the greatest potential for growth, this portfolio invests exclusively in stock funds. Stocks have more frequent price changes than other securities, and along with the opportunity for significant gains, the highest degree of risk. However, it's useful to note that returns on stocks have consistently outpaced inflation for more than 50 years.

Appropriate for investors with the following profile:

Investors with long-term goals (15+ years).

Investors with other investments, outside the Plan, providing adequate diversification.

Those who can ride out frequent shifts in portfolio values.

Those who seek maximum growth.

Those who want the highest potential return from a long term investment.

Asset Mix: 100% Equity

Kinds of funds: Equity-Value, Growth, Growth/Income, Small Cap, Foreign

3. Selecting the right mutual fund will take some understanding of the information that the funds send you. To get some practice, call several mutual funds (you should have seen ads for numerous funds with their 800 number when you were doing experiential problem 1 in chapter 14). Request the information packets that they all have available.

When your packet arrives, study it carefully. Ask yourself the following questions.

1. Does this family of funds have a fund that fits my goals? (look back to experiential problem 2 in this chapter.)

2. How has the fund(s) performed in comparison to the S&P 500 or other indexes over the last few years?

3. Is this a large fund? Is a large fund what I want? (There have been numerous articles on the pro's and con's of large funds in recent issues of Fortune, Money Magazine and other publications. You might want to look up some of them.)

4. Is this a large family of funds? Is the ability to move from fund to fund in the same family important to me?

5. What is the Morningstar rating of this fund?

Chapter 15 Solutions

What Do You Know?

1. T
2. F
3. F
4. T
5. T

6. T
7. F
8. T
9. F
10. F

Key Terminology Exercise - Crossword Puzzle

Across
1. distributions
5. prospectus
7. rebalancing
8. open end investment company

Down
1. dollar cost averaging
2. mutual fund family
3. load charges
4. net asset value
6. front end load

Multiple Choice Questions

1. d
2. c
3. b
4. d
5. a
6. c
7. d
8. b
9. e
10. a

11. d
12. d
13. a
14. e
15. c
16. d

Experiential Problems

1a.

1. T-bills
2. money market instruments
3. T-noteT-bonds
4. municipal bonds and corporate bonds (investment grade), mortgage pass-through securities
5. blue chip stocks, income stocks, asset allocation mutual fund
6. growth stocks; defensive stocks, index mutual fund
7. sector mutual funds, cyclical stocks
8. junk bonds
9. speculative stocks
10. real estate
11. options and futures
12. collectibles

This list may vary somewhat from yours. There is no exactly right answer. If you have large differences discuss them with your professor and think about part B of this problem as a possible explanation.

Part 6

Financial Planning for Tomorrow

Chapter 16

Retirement Planning

What Do You Know?

T F 1. I have started saving for retirement.

T F 2. I can receive tax breaks for certain retirement savings.

T F 3. I may need to save $1 million dollars in order to retire with a decent standard of living.

T F 4. Once I'm 65, Medicare will take care of all of my health care costs.

T F 5. Social Security and my company pension will provide enough money for my retirement.

T F 6. I will not need as much income when I retire as when I was working.

T F 7. There will probably be no Social Security for me to collect when I retire.

T F 8. I should invest my retirement money very conservatively.

T F 9. I will be penalized if I don't start drawing out my retirement money by age 70 1/2.

T F 10. A paid-off home should be the cornerstone of every retirement plan.

Chapter 16

Retirement Planning

Chapter Overview

Thinking about any situation 20, 30, or even 40 years before it will happen is difficult to do. But retirement is the one life situation where you will benefit directly and most assuredly if you begin planning that far ahead. After all, the more time you have to invest money before you retire, the less money you will have to save yourself to meet your goals. This chapter will present threats and protection to retirement as well as a timeline for making critical choices. You will calculate how much retirement income you will need and how much you should be saving now.

Chapter Outline

I. Looking Ahead

    A. Threats

        1. inflation

        2. health care expenses

        3. cost of long term care

        4. estate taxes

        5. income taxes

        6. state and local taxes

    B. Protection

        1. employer pension plans

        2. retirement savings plans

        3. Social Security

        4. wise investing and spending

        5. Medicare

        6. health insurance

        7. estate planning

C. A timeline for making important choices

    1. before age 50

        a. start saving for retirement

        b. make sound spending decisions

        c. follow your budget and financial plan

        d. prepare a will

    2. by age 55

        a. develop retirement plan

        b. qualify for one-time capital gains exclusion on home sale

        c. can draw money from retirement plans if you leave your job

    3. by age 65

        a. become eligible for Medicare and Social Security

        b. receive full pension benefits from company

II. Financing Your Retirement

A. Factors that determine your savings needs

    1. age

    2. current income

    3. desired retirement income

    4. current retirement savings

    5. other sources of retirement income

    6. your tax rate (both pre- and post-retirement)

    7. expected rate of inflation

    8. expected return on your retirement savings

B. The lessons when saving for retirement

    1. start early

    2. save as much as you can

    3. use tax deferred retirement savings plans

    4. don't be too conservative when investing for retirement

III. Social Security

A. Understanding the Social Security System

    1. Old Age and Survivors Insurance Fund

    2. Disability Insurance Trust Fund

    3. Hospital Insurance Trust Fund

    4. Supplementary Medical Insurance Trust Fund

    5. opening a Social Security account

    6. applying for benefits

    B. Computing your retirement benefits

        1. average indexed monthly earnings (AIME)

        2. primary insurance amount (PIA)

        3. working after retirement

        4. taxes and Social Security benefits

    C. The future of the Social Security System

IV. Employer Sponsored Retirement Plans

    A. Defined benefit

        1. guaranteed a certain benefit each year upon retirement

        2. example - pension plan

        3. based on employer's income and number of years worked for company

        4. vesting - certain period of service required to receive benefits

    B. Defined contribution plan

        1. no guarantee as to the benefits but the employer guarantees the amount it will contribute

        2. examples - 401(k) and 403(b)

        3. employee has control over where funds are invested

        4. also called salary reduction plans, because it reduces taxable income thereby reducing taxes

        5. contribution limits

        6. vesting - not as long as defined benefit

V. Individual Retirement Plans

    A. Individual retirement accounts (IRA)

        1. any wage earner can set up an IRA

        2. tax savings for some people

        3. unlimited investment options

        4. rollover IRA - investing a lump-sum distribution from a retirement plan

    B. SEP plan

        1. pension plan for small businesses

        2. designed to reduce paperwork

    C. Keogh plan

        1. pension plan for self-employed

        2. can be used by anyone with an outside income source

        3. many Keogh participants have a SEP or an IRA

VI. Receiving Retirement Benefits

    A. Payout options

        1. choice of payout depends on your personal situation

        2. many people choose multiple payout options

    B. Choosing an annuity

        1. rate

        2. commission

        3. withdrawal penalties

        4. rates and annual fees

        5. financial strength of the issuer

VII. Taxes and Your Retirement

    A. Withdrawing money from retirement plans

        1. if you leave your job

        2. age 59 1/2

    B. Limits on the amount you can withdraw

Name _____   Instructor _____

Date _____   Section _____

Key Terminology - Matching

Match the words in column A to the statements in column B.

Column A

A. Old Age and Survivors Insurance Fund

B. Disability Insurance Trust Fund

C. Hospital Insurance Trust Fund

D. Supplementary Medical Insurance Trust Fund

E. AIME

F. PIA

G. PEBES

H. Qualified retirement plan

I. Defined benefit plan

J. Defined contribution plan

K. Vested

L. Keogh plan

Column B

___ 1. Plans where you know how much goes in each year, such as 401(k) and 403(b).

___ 2. A formula, which changes each year, is applied to this to determine your monthly social security benefit.

___ 3. You should request one of these regularly to make sure that your Social Security account is correct.

___ 4. The fund from which your Social Security benefits will be paid when you retire.

___ 5. You must work for an employer for a set number of years to be this.

___ 6. If your pension is a percentage of your salary, you have this.

___ 7. If you begin drawing Social Security retirement benefits early you will receive less than this.

___ 8. If self-employed people wish to build a pension plan, this is a possible option.

___ 9. If you are injured and cannot work, this fund will be very important to you.

___ 10. There are two types of this.

___ 11. This fund is supported by a 2.9% tax on earnings payable by the employee and employer.

Name _____   Instructor _____

Date _____   Section _____

Multiple Choice Questions

1. The amount of income you will need when you retire compared to your income while working will be
   a. much less.
   b. slightly less.
   c. about the same.
   d. more.

2. To retire comfortably, a person in his or her 30's will need to save about what percentage of their annual income?
   a. 10%
   b. 20%
   c. 30%
   d. 40%

3. The most reliable ways to protect your retirement are
   a. government mandated.
   b. controlled by you.
   c. controlled by your employer.
   d. don't really work that well.

4. You need to make specific retirement decisions (when, where, etc.) about age
   a. 30.
   b. 40.
   c. 50.
   d. 60.

5. Huge tax penalties are imposed if you fail to begin making withdrawals from your retirement accounts by age
   a. 59 1/2.
   b. 62.
   c. 65.
   d. 70 1/2.

6. All of the following statements are true about retirement savings **except**
   a. save as much as you can afford.
   b. be conservative.
   c. start early.
   d. take advantage of tax deferred savings plans.
   e. it's never too late to start retirement planning.

7. Social Security covers
    a. 60% of all workers.
    b. 70% of all workers.
    c. 80% of all workers.
    d. 90% of all workers.

8. To begin collecting Social Security, you will need to do all of the following **except**
    a. apply for benefits.
    b. have a passport as proof of identity.
    c. have a birth certificate as proof of eligibility.
    d. have your most recent tax return or W-2.

9. Social Security retirement benefits cannot be collected by
    a. a retired worker.
    b. the dependent spouse of a retired worker.
    c. the dependent children of a retired worker.
    d. the dependent parents of a retired worker.

10. Due to the changes that will probably take place in regards to Social Security, you should count on Social Security in your retirement income as
    a. only a small percentage.
    b. an increasing percentage.
    c. a large percentage.
    d. no part since it will probably not exist when you retire.

11. A qualified retirement plan
    a. offers tax advantages to the employer and employee.
    b. is a defined benefit plan.
    c. is a defined contribution plan.
    d. all of the above

12. Which of the following are examples of defined contribution plans?
    a. 401(k)
    b. 403(b)
    c. SEP plan
    d. a and b, only

13. An individual can set up all of the following plans not tied to any employer **except**
    a. 403(b).
    b. IRA.
    c. Keogh plan.
    d. b and d, only

14. The tax deductibility of contributions to an IRA are determined by
    a. your income.
    b. your marital status.
    c. how much your employer contributes.
    d. a and b, only

15. The best retirement distribution option is
    a. whatever best suits the individual's needs.
    b. annuity.
    c. periodic payments.
    d. lump sum.

Name _____   Instructor _____

Date _____   Section _____

Experiential Problems

1. This Quiz is designed to help you decide where to invest your retirement plan dollars. Use this tool in combination with other investment and retirement planning advice available to you.

    To complete: After each question, circle the number that best reflects your answer. Your total score will point to a sample portfolio that may be right for you.

    1. **Investment Emphasis/Need**
        "When it comes to my retirement account, I'm looking for..."
        - 4 Maximum Growth
        - 3 Growth
        - 2 Growth & Income
        - 1 Income

    2. **Time Horizon**
        "I expect to start using my retirement plan money in..."
        - 4 More than 15 years
        - 3 11 to 15 years
        - 2 6 to 10 years
        - 1 less than 5 years

    3. **Return Expectations**
        "In pursuit of higher long-term returns, I'm willing to accept annual returns that may vary greatly."
        - 4 Strongly Agree
        - 3 Agree
        - 2 Agree Somewhat
        - 1 Disagree

    4. **Risk Tolerance**
        "I'm willing to tolerate a short-term decline in the value of my retirement account if that's what it takes to achieve potentially higher long-term returns."
        - 4 Strongly Agree
        - 3 Agree
        - 2 Agree Somewhat
        - 1 Disagree

    5. **Liquidity Needs**
        "I don't expect to use money from my retirement account prior to retiring (e.g., for college expenses or home purchases)."
        - 4 Strongly Agree
        - 3 Agree
        - 2 Agree Somewhat
        - 1 Disagree

    6. **Financial "IQ"**
        "I consider my knowledge of investing and personal money management to be..."
        - 4 Very High
        - 3 High
        - 2 Medium
        - 1 Low

    7. **Inflation Concern**
        "My level of concern over the future impact of inflation on my investment returns is..."
        - 4 Very High
        - 3 High
        - 2 Medium
        - 1 Low

    _____ **Total Points**

Model Portfolios	
Allocation	**Range of Annual Returns***

Conservative (7-10 points)

20% Money Market		Low	1.6%
80% Bond		Average	5.7%
		High	9.7%

Moderately Conservative (11-14 points)

10% Money Market		Low	-1.5%
10% International Equity		Average	8.3%
40% Bond		High	18.0%
40% Managed			

Conservative Growth (15-19 points)

10% Aggressive Growth		Low	-3.9%
10% International Equity		Average	11.3%
20% Managed		High	26.5%
30% Bond			
30% Growth & Income			

Moderately Aggressive (20-24 points)

20% Aggressive Growth		Low	-7.0%
20% Bond		Average	18.3%
20% Growth & Income		High	34.3%
20% Growth			
20% International Equity			

Aggressive (25-28 points)

20% Growth		Low	-17.7%
20% International Equity		Average	18.0%
		High	53.7%

*Based on these Funds

Account	**Invests In**	**Account**	**Invests In**
Money Market	Money Market	Bond	Scudder S T-Bond
Managed	Fidelity Puritan	Growth & Inc.	Warburg Pincus G&I
Growth	Fidelity Contra	Agg. Growth	PBHG Growth
Int'l Equity	Templeton Foreign		

2. What effect does waiting to start saving for retirement have on how much you will need to save or how much you will eventually have? This problem will illustrate very dramatically the answer to this question. (Hint: Use the Worksheet "Calculating Your Retirement Nest Egg" as a guide.)

   a. Assume that you will need to save $750,000 by age 65. Using 5% as your expected real rate of return and assuming you have no current retirement savings, compute what you will need to save each year to reach your goal if you begin saving at age ___.

      1) 25 (Table B 40 years at 5% = 120.79)

      2) 35

      3) 45

      4) 55

   b. Assume that you can save $7,000 per year at 5%. How much of a retirement nest egg will you have if you start saving at age ___?

      1) 25

      2) 35

      3) 45

      4) 55

   c. Review your answers in a and b and answer the question posed in the beginning of this problem.

3. The authors suggest that you not be overly conservative with your retirement investments. Rework problem #2, but instead of 5% use 8% as your expected real rate of return. Is there much of a change in your answers?

    a. 1) 25 (Table 40 years at 8% = 259.05)

        2) 35

        3) 45

        4) 55

    b. 1) 25

        2) 35

        3) 45

        4) 55

Chapter 16 Solutions

What Do You Know?

1. T	6. F
2. T	7. F
3. T	8. F
4. F	9. T
5. F	10. F

Key Terminology Exercise - Matching

1. J	6. I
2. E	7. F
3. G	8. L
4. A	9. B
5. K	10. H
	11. C

Multiple Choice Questions

1. c	11. d
2. a	12. d
3. b	13. d
4. c	14. d
5. d	15. a
6. b	
7. d	
8. b	
9. d	
10. a	

Experiential Problems

1. results vary per individual

2. a. 1) $750,000 / 120.79 = $6,209 required annual savings
      2) $750,000 / 66.4388 = $11,289 required annual savings
      3) $750,000 / 33.0660 = $22,682 required annual savings
      4) $750,000 / 12.5779 = $59,628 required annual savings

   b. 1) $7,000 x 120.79 = $845,530 retirement nest egg
      2) $7,000 x 66.4338 = $465,072 retirement nest egg
      3) $7,000 x 33.0660 = $231,462 retirement nest egg
      4) $7,000 x 12.5779 = $ 88,045 retirement nest egg

3. a. 1) $750,000 / 259.05 = $2,895 required annual savings
      2) $750,000 / 113.2832 = $6,621 required annual savings
      3) $750,000 / 45.7620 = $16,389 required annual savings
      4) $750,000 / 14.4866 = $51,772 required annual savings

   b. 1) $7,000 x 259.05 = $1,813,140 retirement next egg
      2) $7,000 x 113.2832 = $792,982 retirement nest egg
      3) $7,000 x 45.7620 = $320,334 retirement nest egg
      4) $7,000 x 14.4866 = $101,406 retirement nest egg

Chapter 17

Estate Planning

What Do You Know?

T F   1. Every adult, regardless of age, should have a will.

T F   2. Leaving all your property to your spouse can save a lot of money on taxes.

T F   3. If you're young, with no money and little children, you have no need of estate planning.

T F   4. Only rich people need wills.

T F   5. Doing your own estate planning is a wise decision.

T F   6. Jointly owned property could automatically bypass your will.

T F   7. Giving away part of your estate while you're still alive reduces the estate taxes.

T F   8. A living will ensures that your wishes about medical treatment will be carried out.

T F   9. Unless you have over $50,000 you should not consider setting a trust.

T F 10. I have a will.

Chapter 17

Estate Planning

Chapter Overview

Estate planning might sound like a topic for millionaires. But if you own any property or have children and don't want strangers making decisions for you, estate planning is something you need to do. Although it sounds complicated, a competent attorney can greatly assist you in understanding and setting up the necessary components. Some of the tasks you will need to consider are: preparing a will; granting power of attorney should you become disabled; appointing a guardian and conservator for your minor children.

Procrastinating about these decisions will not postpone your death, but merely transfer the power of these decisions to someone else.

Chapter Outline

I. Understanding Estate Planning

    A. Contents and value of an estate

        1. calculate the value of assets and liabilities
        2. use fair market value
        3. ownership forms

            a. joint tenants with rights of survivorship
            b. power of attorney

    B. Goals of estate planning

        1. to minimize taxes
        2. to declare who gets what of your property
        3. to name who will care for your minor children

II. Estates and Taxes

    A. Federal taxes

        1. none owed if estate is worth less than $600,000
        2. bequests to charities and spouse pass along tax free
        3. tax is progressive
        4. tax is paid by the estate, not the beneficiaries
        5. none owed if you skip a generation and pass $1 million to grandchildren

6. extra taxes may be due on excess accumulations

7. estate taxes are due within nine months of your death

B. State taxes

1. some states have an estate tax

2. 50% of states have an inheritance tax

C. Saving money on taxes

1. leave everything to spouse

2. establish a trust

3. give away your property

4. make charitable contributions

III. Wills

A. The probate system

1. probate is the legal processing of wills upon death

2. intestate - dying without a will

B. The types and contents of a will

1. individual will

2. joint will

3. formally drawn will

4. holographic will

5. must be signed, dated, and witnessed

6. codicil - minor changes to will

7. identification

8. debt payment

9. property distribution

10. trusts

11. executor

12. guardian

13. funeral arrangements

C. Selecting a guardian

1. if you don't select someone to care for your children, the courts will

2. conservator - makes financial decisions for your children until they are of legal age

D. Last letter of instruction - some specifics regarding your property

    E. Living wills

        1. states your intent for your care should you become unable to do so

        2. ignored by some doctors and hospitals

IV. Trusts

    A. Four purposes

        1. manage money of a minor

        2. limit the way the beneficiary can use the money

        3. provide tax advantages

        4. avoid probate and public scrutiny of estate

    B. Testamentary trusts - written into will and becomes operative at death

    C. Living trust - appoints a trustee to handle assets while person is living

    D. Life estate - variation of a living trust

    E. Insurance trusts - administers proceeds of life insurance

V. Gifts

    A. Taxes and gifts - up to $10,000 per year per recipient

    B. Gifts to minors

        1. irrevocable

        2. anything over $1,200 taxed at the parent's tax rate

        3. could ultimately reduce amount of college financial aid for child

    C. Other types of gifts

        1. unlimited gifts to spouse

        2. gifts to charities capped at a % of AGI

Name _____   Instructor _____

Date _____   Section _____

Key Terminology Exercise - Fill In

1. Odd as it may sound, if you do not spend enough of your money while alive, especially if it is in qualified retirement plans, you may reduce what your heirs receive because of taxes on the _____.

2. If you are single you can only be the _____ of a(n) _____ but if married you can also have a(n) _____.

3. To make sure you get buried where and how you want, you should leave a detailed _____.

4. Although most commonly used by married couples, business partners may also own property as _____.

5. Soldiers in Desert Storm gave _____ to spouses, parents or a close friend to enable their business affairs to be handled for them while they were in the Middle East.

6. When grandpa sets a savings account for his new granddaughter's college education, it is done so under the _____.

7. If you are unhappy with your family and wish to ''get even'' with them after you are dead, die _____ and let them fight over your estate.

8. Only an attorney can do a _____ but you can do your own _____.

9. To insure that you will be taken care of should you be unable to communicate, a _____ with your instructions and a _____ to provide the funds are essential.

10. When a will is submitted to _____ after a person's death, one of the first actions is to determine the _____ of the assets.

11. A handwritten _____ to a will is often times the reason a will is contested.

12. If you wish to provide money for your minor children's college education, a _____ written into your will is one way to accomplish it.

Name _____   Instructor _____

Date _____   Section _____

Multiple Choice Questions

1. You need to be concerned with estate planning when
    a. you become wealthy.
    b. you become old.
    c. you have children.
    d. you become of legal age.

2. If property is owned jointly by business partners and one dies, how much of the property value goes to the estate of the deceased?
    a. the entire value
    b. one half the value
    c. none of it
    d. depends on the partnership agreement

3. The reason(s) for estate planning is (are)
    a. to minimize federal and state taxes.
    b. to distribute your estate after you die.
    c. to distribute your estate before you die.
    d. all of the above

4. If your estate is under $600,000 you will not need to be concerned with
    a. probate.
    b. federal estate taxes.
    c. having a will.
    d. a and c, only

5. All of the following are excluded from your estate **except**
    a. real estate.
    b. proceeds of life insurance policies.
    c. amounts in qualified retirement plans.
    d. all of the above

6. Retirees must be concerned with estate taxes in another state if
    a. they draw a pension from a company in that state.
    b. they lived in the state at the time they drew their will.
    c. they own property in the state.
    d. a and b, only

7. The best ways to save money on estate taxes include all of the following **except**
   a. leave everything to your spouse and children.
   b. set up a qualified trust that doubles your $600,000 exemption.
   c. give away your property.
   d. make charitable contributions.

8. All of the following are true about wills **except**
   a. all adults should have one.
   b. once written, they are good for life.
   c. it is simple and inexpensive to create one.
   d. a and c, only

9. If you die without a will
   a. Uncle Sam could be the big winner in estate taxes collected
   b. the court will decide who gets your property.
   c. it could take years to settle your estate.
   d. all of the above

10. The payments that are made by an estate are:
    1. bequests to beneficiaries
    2. probate costs
    3. federal and state estate taxes

    The order in which they are paid is
    a. 2, 1, 3.
    b. 2, 3, 1.
    c. 3, 2, 1.
    d. 3, 1, 2.

11. The Uniform Probate Codes is designed to give the primary responsibility for settling an estate to
    a. the courts.
    b. statutory law.
    c. the family.
    d. all of the above

12. It is almost impossible to exclude who from your will?
    a. spouse
    b. children
    c. parents
    d. all of the above

13. A last letter of instruction is all of the following **except**
    a. prepared in addition to a will.
    b. contains funeral and burial instructions.
    c. describes how to divide you property.
    d. is legally binding.

14. A living will
    a. relieves loved ones of the burden of making life and death decisions.
    b. expresses your wishes to refuse extraordinary medical treatment.
    c. can not be ignored by doctors.
    d. a and b, only

15. A trust performs which of the following purposes?
    a. manages the money of a minor
    b. limits how a beneficiary can use the money
    c. provides tax advantages
    d. all of the above

16. Living trusts are all of the following **except**
    a. a way to avoid probate.
    b. fairly easy to set up.
    c. easier to contest than a will.
    d. provides for easy distribution of assets at death.

Name _____ Instructor _____

Date _____ Section _____

Experiential Problems

1. One of the first steps in estate planning should be to estimate the value of your estate. Fill out the following worksheet. Don't forget to redo this worksheet every few years or when you have a major change in your personal assets.

Worksheet Estimating the Value of Your Estate

Estate Contents

1. Primary residence	
2. Other real estate	
3. Securities (stocks, bonds, mutual funds)	
4. Bank accounts	
5. Interest and dividends owed but not paid	
6. Tangible personal property (e.g., automobiles)	
7. Life insurance policies	
8. Annuities paid by contract or agreement	
9. No fault insurance payments owed you	
10. Value of all qualified retirement plans (including IRAs)	
11. Pension death benefits	
12. Income tax refunds	
13. Forgiven debts	
14. UTMA accounts	
15. Closely held businesses	
16. Other items	
Total value of items listed above	
(Funeral Expenses)	
(Costs of settling estate)	
(Unpaid debts)	
Estate Value	

Note - for lines 2, 3, 4, 6, and 7 prepare a detailed inventory list of the items in each category.

2.   Just as every adult should have a will, so also should they have a letter of last instructions. Although not the most fun topic to consider, how you wish your funeral and burial to be conducted must be dealt with. Give the topic some thought and write a letter of last instructions below.

3. More and more people are using video tape to create a living will. Find out the legal requirements for a video living will in your state. Once you know how one needs to be prepared, you may want to find a camcorder (your schools AV Department may have them available for student use) and prepare a living will.

Chapter 17 Solutions

What Do You Know?

1. T
2. T
3. F
4. F
5. F
6. T
7. T
8. F
9. F
10. T

Key Terminology Exercise - Fill In

1. excess accumulation
2. testator, individual will, joint will
3. last letter of instructions
4. joint tenants with right of survivorship
5. power of attorney
6. Uniform Transfer to Minors Act
7. intestate
8. formally drawn will, holographic will
9. living will, living trust
10. probate, fair market value
11. codicil
12. testamentary trust

Multiple Choice Questions

1. d
2. a
3. d
4. b
5. d
6. c
7. a
8. b
9. d
10. b
11. c
12. a
13. d
14. d
15. d
16. c